"I'm a working title that's for sure…"

Light & Love
Nathaniel M. Gray

Copyright © 2020 Nathan Gray
Published by Dark Gospel Transmissions
in partnership with End Hits Records
All rights reserved.
ISBN 978-0-578-62631-4

||| Preface |||

||| 1 |||
Face down is where you'll need to make your peace
In the ashes of what once was everything

||| 2 |||
The burns will form a scar around your pain
A monument to where you lost your faith
And rose again to fight another day
And fall again to never be the same

||| 3 |||
There is a light where the darkness feels no shame
There is a love that never has to fade

||| 4 |||
Black out, wake up, start swinging, face the pain
Failures come and go but that's OK

||| 5 |||
Prepare for war don't let them under your skin
Remember where you've come from where you've been
And rose again to fight another day
And fall again to never be the same

||| 6 |||
Yeah, there is a light where the darkness feels no shame
There is a love that never has to fade

To: The Lovers, The Dreamers, and Me.

PREFACE

"Life or death...the choice is always ours."

  I will assume that if you hold this book in your hands now, you have read through my journey in *Until The Darkness Takes Us,* an autobiographical purging that spilled out of me desperately during a time of deep personal transformation.
  I sometimes feel as though I live entire lifetimes in the span of a single year. As I look back on all that has happened since the release of *Until The Darkness Takes Us,* I feel a crossroads of emotion somewhere between pride and utter exhaustion. Between peace and wanting more. The last three years since that book was published have been incredibly eye-opening, and I have learned and grown so much; ever evolving into the man I am meant to be. I firmly believe that evolution is the greatest gift of life - we are not only capable of change, it is our right and our duty to do so. Through success and failure, The Becoming is constant, and experiencing (not just surviving) both is how we genuinely grow.
  Where I was when *Until The Darkness Takes Us* left off was a place in which I felt incredibly strong and empowered. I had gone through a great shedding of emotional weight and naively assumed that I was where and who I was going to be. Admittedly, shortly thereafter, I fell off a proverbial cliff and, when the high of that release wore off, I bottomed out. I had come to realize that instead of trusting that I knew what was best for me, I was searching for answers and validation in everything and everyone around me. As I look back now, it should have been no surprise that my mental and physical

health plummeted into an alarmingly unstable place.

<u>I was still living in the darkness.</u>

Through intense self-reflection and saying "no" to people, habits, ideals and environments that did not serve me, I am proud to say that I fought my way out of the darkness and am truly working towards peace. Make no mistake, I still struggle every single day, but I now know how to get back up because I realize that the importance lies in the simple act of Just Getting The Fuck Back Up. Failure is *always* an option. Failure is human. It is inevitable. But failure is also a gift because it is part of the process of growing and healing. I think finding comfortability in that is what gives us the opportunity to be great.

If you were expecting to pick this book up and read through a glorified track-by-track of my newest album, I am sorry to say that you will be disappointed. *Light & Love* is a deep dive into the darkest places of my heart and mind - the places from which my albums *Feral Hymns, Working Title* and the EP between them were born. It is messy and painful and real.

My transformation musically, emotionally, physically and spiritually all came back to one simple truth:

Everyone and everything I thought I needed to be, I already was...

... and I have so much more to say.

Face down is where you'll need to make your peace

In the ashes of what once was everything

The Afterword

When I started writing *Until The Darkness Takes Us*, I knew that a large and dreadful part of my past was going to go public. I also knew that it was well beyond time for me to share the experience of my abuse into the world. My hope was that giving my story life beyond the darkest corners of my mind would help relieve a crushing weight from my lungs, after which my healing could finally begin. I wrote those chapters in such a way that danced around the words, draping them in artfully crafted, almost poetic statements. Part of me wanted to just say the words "I was sexually abused as a child" outright; the other part was terrified that doing so would somehow make the affliction of my stigmata more real. I admit that I was also tiptoeing around the subject a bit, worried about opening the doors to those dark corners that I had been keeping locked so tightly. Shortly before the book was released though (11 days before, to be exact), I woke with the memories suffocating me more than usual, and I decided to say the words aloud in a live video for thousands to see all at once. I suppose I felt that there was a bit of control I could maintain over how it was received if I could ensure that, on one specific day, everyone who knew me would know what had happened to me. The purging came quite frantically, with me sitting in front of my computer, hitting the "go live" button on my Facebook page and, in what felt like a dream sequence, the words just started spilling out of me. The time somehow went by lightning fast and agonizingly slow all at once.

Almost immediately, the comments, telephone calls, texts and private messages came pouring in. One after another, after another. As I sat in the aftermath, trying to come to terms with what I had just said and done, teetering through dizzying panic, it occurred to me that I had not only just unburdened my heart; I had connected with a tragic amount of others who had lived through similar horrors. It was as if suddenly I belonged to a club – one whose membership price none of us ever volunteered to pay, and of whose horrible ranks we never wanted to be a part. It seemed as though for every one heartfelt message of sympathy I received, there was another of shared, tragic understanding. My father had lovingly and immediately driven to be with me. I remember sitting in my living room with him a few hours after the purging and setting my phone aside on silent because I had absolutely no idea how to respond to the outpouring of encouragement. Those first few days I had to purposefully pace my reading of the notes because I was quite honestly overwhelmed by love, grief, hope, shame and a myriad other emotions that I am still to this day unable to describe.

    I was, and still am, eternally grateful for the support gifted to me throughout this particular unveiling. That said (and I discovered after talking to other survivors of similar brands of trauma that I am not alone in this), I felt intense guilt that I was wildly undeserving of such adoration and celebration. Freely accepting support is often much more difficult than it sounds. My subconscious mind was ringing with the notion that I was tainted, damaged and unworthy. Beyond that, I often put the pressure on myself by thinking that no matter what response I give to such messages, it may not be good enough. I would never want to simply take and hold onto your stories of abuse or your amazingly sweet messages of support. I want you to understand and feel that they were received with my whole heart. I often struggle with how to verbalize my gratitude and feel a certain duty or responsibility to inspire you in return. It's taken me a bit of time to balance the idea that someone would be offended or feel slighted if I don't respond immediately, with the need to take time to sit with the energy someone has given me and responding with what I can, when I can - no more, no less.

It has been three years since I went public with my affliction, and I still receive messages of support nearly weekly. Tragically, after almost every show I have played since then, I have hugged another new person who has shared their Me Too with me. I hate it for all of us, but am so glad that we no longer suffer alone in silence.

Perhaps I had convinced myself that I was "all better" once my story had been told and felt a bit of false comfort. It was much like that feeling after a good long cry where you are exhausted, but relieved of some great weight. In all honesty, all I had really done was release some emotions that were tied to a terrible thing that had happened to me. I didn't actually fix or change anything in my mind or soul with the release of those emotions, so it should have been no surprise to me that once that post-cry high wore off, I'd be right back where I started. Just…publicly.

The first few times I found myself shrouded in darkness again after that unveiling, I became consumed with the feelings of guilt and shame. There may even have been some disappointment in myself. I had done this huge, terrifying, freeing thing, and I wanted to be all better. I wanted to be free from being triggered into awful places. I wanted the upper hand. Answers. SOMETHING. What I have learned about myself since then is immeasurable. I've learned not to let myself believe each time I fall will be the last time. Not to believe that every good day will go without bottoming out. I've learned to embrace the ups and downs while recognizing that both are subject to change direction at a moment's notice - and that that is OK. It reminds me of a quote by Barack Obama, "Better is good." We should work for better, not perfection.

Most importantly though, I've learned that true strength is just getting the fuck back up when I fall. Strength is forgiving myself. It is in the humility and humbleness that comes only after I've risen from my darkest times. It's in survival and personal victory in whatever way any of us may define it for ourselves. It's in accepting our failures as wholly as we do our victories. I have never spent a moment in regret that I went public because I know the ramifications of keeping my pain in, and I don't ever want to make that mistake again. Perhaps that's why this book was so important for me to write. I want to continue the work and hope to inspire others to do the same. Heroes are born from these baptisms by fire. You…me. Us.

My healing has not been easy, but it has been constant. I am ever-grateful for the people in my life who have pushed and pulled me along through it. The people who challenge me when I need it, love me when I don't deserve it, and sit quietly with me when I can't stop spinning. Those who tell me no. Those who tell me yes. Those who cheerlead and celebrate me with full enthusiasm, and those who boo and jeer me much the same.

And, of course, you – who may be all or none of those things. I'm glad you're here.

The burns will form a scar around your pain

A monument to where you lost your faith

And rose again to fight another day

And fall again to never be the same

From "Solo" to <u>Solo</u>

The year that *Until The Darkness Take Us* came out was hands down one of my most intense years to date. 2017 was an absolute roller coaster, with the highest highs and lowest lows. The year began with the debut of both the book and album, each of which I decided should be self-released because - why not? Getting those two things out into the world (at the same time, no less!) was more work and chaos than I could have ever anticipated it would have been. Dan and I, along with a couple of dedicated friends, worked our asses off day and night putting together every single piece of the machine that went into the creation of the book and album, and their subsequent birth into the world. I learned more about the industry during that time than I had in my previous 20 years combined as an artist. In the end, it was amazing to be able to say, "We did this on our own." Utterly exhausting, but amazing.

Just after the release of the album, Dan and I, along with Jake Blochinger, a drummer who I had met through my friends at Good Fight Records, headed out to Europe to tour as Nathan Gray Collective. I remember that tour as just being so much fun, and it kept my mind off a lot of not-fun shit brewing under the surface. Jake, an energetic young kid from Jersey, balanced me and Dan perfectly in terms of personality, and that whole run of shows was a blast. If you were to marry The Casting Out and I AM HERESY, you would get a Nathan Gray Collective show. Every single night was a ritual - we set the stage with sigils, candles and other dark imagery; and there was a strangely perfect mix of fun dance-driven songs and all out dark symphonic pieces. Every night, we would end the set with the song "Corson," which we had made more intense for the live show. I would go completely insane - screaming in a full-on rage-induced fit, working out my own fear, anger, hatred and disgust. Wax and bones would fly across the stage, peppering us, the equipment and any innocent bystander in the front row. That tour really allowed me a place to hide behind the internal chaos I was working through, while also allowing me the very necessary opportunity to hang out safely with friends after exorcising such intense emotions. On stage, I was showing specific emotions to the world (such as anger) as a bit of a front while I battled internally to find who I thought I was, or even attempt to discover what emotion I was suppressing inside me. At the time, I mistook this display of anger as a sign of strength. I recognize now that it wasn't strength at all; it was just posturing as I tried masking my hurt. It took me a little bit to come to the realization that calm acceptance and knowing when to be still with your thoughts is true strength. Acting out and raging was just a way to block my emotions. If I'm screaming - on stage, on the internet, or in the streets – it is most often a distraction from some deeper problem at hand.

Dan and I were incredible partners when it came to writing and playing music, but in the business of, well, BUSINESS, we had vastly different styles. This began to strain our longstanding friendship, which neither of us wanted. I tend to be a bit chaotic and habitually urgent, and he needs order and well-laid plans. The stress was no fault of either of ours, and I don't doubt that going through the process of self-releasing the album played a huge part in it. I remember Dan asking me over one day for a conversation about the future of Nathan Gray Collective; it was actually very easy to agree that it made sense to just stop being in a band together, at least for the foreseeable future. We left it with absolutely no hard feelings whatsoever (I was even in his wedding this past fall) and he and I went our separate musical ways.

I know that people generally look at me and think

that I must be confident, self-assured and intentional - there's always a bit of laughter when I confess that The Casting Out was created when I chickened out trying to go solo. The truth is, I struggle hard with my inner critic. My self-worth is a battle I fight in all areas of life. Even music. There is a part of me that believes that my creativity was born from my brokenness and is not a natural, inherent ability. So I struggle to understand what part of who I am is just me and what part of me is what was born from the abuse. This battle is certainly irrational, and a thing that literally does not matter in the grand scheme of my life. What matters is that I have creativity at all. I couldn't even really tell you *why* I might feel as "less than" if one were more true than the other (or which would feel more valid to me); I suppose in part, it's that my story is so connectable and inspirational, I worry about this being unintentionally dishonest.

     Looking back over my musical journey, it is obvious to me now that I was continually looking to others over the years to help me fill my self-perceived musical gaps. I was living in fear and doubt of my abilities, which meant that I needed to do my own thing at that point of my life more than ever before. I had to cut the bullshit, stop wallowing in my "I'm not good enough" manner of thinking and just take that proverbial leap of faith. Easier said than done, of course. In every band I've ever been in, I would pick at a guitar and pass an idea to Dan, or someone in boysetsfire or The Casting Out to have them make it better. Polishing turds, if you will. "Deja Coup" was exactly that - it was my idea channeled through Chad. I had come to him and said, "I want to do a song like this," and proceeded to crudely play it out on a guitar and give him some vocal noises to show how I heard it. He, of course, took it and made it the incredible piece it is today. boysetsfire is very much a collaboration of ideas, and we always joke that you can't claim you wrote a song unless you could play every single part of it on your own.

After Dan and I put Nathan Gray Collective on the shelf, I honestly had no formal plan or intent for my "what next?". I was starting to feel extremely unwell mentally and physically and had no energy or direction for what I would do next musically, or otherwise. I carried on with life as usual: father and husband by day, man plucking away at guitar on couch at night. I had no inclination that there were some huge life shifts ahead (again).

A Midsummers Night Collapse

By my 45th birthday that year, I was struggling mentally and wearing the effects of it physically. I can sit here and scroll through old photos and tell you exactly where I was mentally based on my body. Too thin? Anxious. Too round? Depressed. Just the other day, I was staring at a photo of myself from that June - belly swollen, bags under my eyes - and I almost felt woozy with the memory of how that summer felt. Everywhere I went, the air felt heavy with conflict and stress and sadness. Uncertainty. Doubt. Fear. That summer, my body started to shut down. My stomach felt like it was eating itself at all times. My muscles ached. Heartburn made it painful to eat or drink. There was joint pain. Back pain. Headaches DAILY. I never slept well. There were visits to doctors and treatment of disruptive symptoms, but I didn't yet understand that all I was feeling physically was directly related to the critical situation of my mental health. So, I just kept declining, plummeting towards my newest rock bottom.

The only time I can recall being even deeper in the pit of depression and madness than this was while trying to navigate life alone in Richmond. I was away from the only place that felt like home to me. I had uprooted myself for the wrong person, and once it inevitably went south, I basically challenged myself to make it work in this new place. I felt it was better to suffer than admit to family and friends that I had made a horrible mistake leaving home. I fell apart fast. I quit showing up to work, stopped paying rent, and my days consisted of nothing more than drinking and self-destruction with some occasional writing peppered in. Classic "tortured artist" bullshit. When I wrote "Quixote's Last Ride," I was sitting on the couch one morning, drinking a poisonous concoction of some sort of alcoholic blend and picking away at the guitar. Lying next to me just a half-cushion away was a gun, begging me to pick it up and put it in my mouth… and that morning I was fucking listening to it. Eventually, the mindless strumming my fingers were doing while I was fantasizing about tasting cold metal began taking on a form. I felt that rush of creativity where it feels like all corners of me are folding up into one another to put focus on nothing but this one song, and it had to be right now. "Quixote" just started coming out of me, and it let me transfer that desperate emotion and suicidal bleakness into art. Songs are special pieces of me like that; understanding me and speaking through me, while holding me in their arms and standing tall, protecting me from the whole world. In this one very real moment, a song saved my life. As The Casting Out songs were written and grew to take on life, there was a weird dichotomy of upbeat songs with horribly depressing lyrics. The stories were both happy and sad; hopeful and melancholic lullabies that aimed to turn negative experiences into positive lessons learned. I guess, in essence, that is a 360-degree representation of me. Leaving Richmond was one of the best decisions of my life. I very vividly remember driving back home after several months had gone by. I pulled up to the condo where my now wife Katie lived at the time and she sprinted out of the house and leapt directly into my arms. Peace. I could breathe again.

Everything about the summer Nathan Gray Collective ended was the same kind of feeling - heavy and suffocating. I was dragging down the people who loved me and spending far too much time ensnared in a toxic web of madness that made me question my sanity in a very precise and wicked way. I have often questioned if I had grown comfortable in my darkness, and I think all of those negative feelings just became normal over the years. I often ended up relinquishing control to my emotional states because there was an odd comfort in just handing over the reins and giving them power over me. It was much easier than fighting them. I'm learning how to challenge that now by starving the parts of myself that crave those negative feelings, while using some discernment to decide which of them provide safety and which provide poison. To be very frank, some of those emotions are doing pretty important work to protect me. Blindly and lazily accepting things like sadness, anger and anxiety as "who I am," however, would be leaning on them as an excuse - they are things we *feel*, not things we ARE. The thought of being what the world may perceive as normal is boring to me, and I can't imagine myself normal... it sounds awful. Creatives like myself are generally anything but. Almost no one creates art from just their happiest places, and yet, when we create, we move people deeply anyway.

Our idiosyncrasies are not the problem. The way we tend to let them control our actions within our daily life CAN be a problem if we don't harness and channel them correctly, though. We can have love, compassion and patience for ourselves while honestly admitting that we need to be better. My hope is that more people learn to love themselves for who and where they are, while being mindful to always call themselves on their own bullshit. My hope is that I can learn to do the same with some form of grace.

Diary of a Madman

Are you ready to hear some wild shit? There is a screaming in my head. A buzzing. It's not so much something I hear as something I feel, and I would not describe it as something good or calming. Sometimes it feels like a pack of wolves howling at the moon - tortuous and awful. At best, it can be likened to cats meowing for food. Something in the farthest corners of my mind is begging me to pay attention to it. It ebbs and flows as if it is getting fed or satiated somehow, although I cannot pinpoint what it may be feeding upon. It has always frightened me. As I have grown older, I have tried to take a psychological interest in it to understand it more, which will hopefully one day disarm whatever it may be. Admittedly, this clinical approach also helps it seem less scary and weird. A lot of my exhaustion mentally and physically comes from trying to block that out, but I don't know that I want to uncover it completely for fear it is shielding something that needs its protection more than I need peace and quiet. I couldn't exactly tell you when it started (or how), just that it's been there as long as I can remember. I don't know how to tend to that noise just yet - but I want to focus on it. At the very least, I want to let it know I feel/hear it, pat its head, say hello and carry on.

This may come as no surprise after hearing that, but I also experience obsessive thought patterns and behaviors. I know…shocker, right? It was much worse when I was younger, but I've still retained a lot of that brand of crazy. A lot. For instance, if my hand accidentally bumps or touches one side of something, I must balance out and bump the other hand, too. I also sometimes get stuck in a horrifying game of "what if" with myself – what if that car hits me, what if this bridge collapses, what if I choke and no one is around to help? I obsess over the thought until the danger becomes real to me, and then I start to panic and don't know why because I don't realize that I've been circling this "what if" in the back of my mind.

In addition to all of THAT, I have a really persistent and unreasonable fear of being poisoned. When I was about 10 years old (in the early 1980's), there was a story in the news about some people who died after taking Tylenol that they later found out was laced with cyanide. To this day, you will not get me to take medicine of any kind without a fight. If you DO somehow get me to do it, it will not be done without a crushing panic attack immediately after. My brain will set itself on doom mode and I will freak out about the fact that I am no longer in control of what happens next because if I HAD just been poisoned, there was no way to get it out of me. I experience similar psychoses with packaged food and bottles of water:

Open bottle. Close bottle. Shake bottle. Take a tiny sip. Wait 15 minutes to ensure I am not going to immediately die from the poison I have just inexplicably shaken up from the bottom of said bottle and then subsequently ingested. Have 15 minutes actually passed? Yes. Decide I will make it to see another day.
Drink rest of water. Carry on.

I think I'm (probably?) not COMPLETELY insane because I know when my behaviors are crazy. Crazy people don't know they are crazy, right? I absolutely know when I'm acting like a madman. More often than not, after calling myself on it, I feel intensely ashamed for being that way. It's sort of like watching myself from the outside, similar to sleep paralysis or locking your keys in the car. You know what I mean, right? When you park the car, get out and, while you are in the act of closing the car door, you see your keys still dangling from the ignition. But there you are…still closing the door anyway while telling yourself, "dammit, don't do it!" But you do. It's sort of like that.

I guess it's important to me to share this side of who I am in a continued effort to just be still. Or rather, be comfortable with stillness. I know I share these oddities of mine almost flippantly, but this whole journey is largely about releasing myself from all the secrets weighing me down. *Everything* I've ever been ashamed of was piling up in my heart until I could barely function under its crushing weight, and, dammit, I want better for my Second Act. I want to know that I was not alone and that people will understand me, hear me, see me, and know that in spite of everything, I still survived. I want them to know that if they find we share a brand of crazy, they will survive, too. Although I find it difficult to imagine anyone else in the world experiencing this sort of madness, if you do, I hope you find your voice to speak up, too. Perhaps we will find strength in numbers.

My Mahnkers & Me

When I was young, I had a bit of a stuffed animal obsession. I had a collection of them that I adored, giving them space in my bed even up to around age 15. There was Waldo (a little stuffed panda), Floppy Dog and Purple Dog, and Joey, who was my favorite doll even after I fucked up his hair by giving him a trim. My mom even made him a new shirt when the one that he came in wore out. There was also my snuggly that I called Cloud Blanket. They served as my guardians and friends, and I talked to them as if they were living, breathing beings. If neighborhood kids came over and accidentally knocked them over, I'd be very upset and carefully line them back up after ensuring that they were OK. To this day, and probably to my wife's chagrin, I am a complete push-over when one of my kids begs me for a stuffed animal toy.

I definitely had some darker protectors as well - Monsters (which my mother will confirm I mispronounced in my childish tongue as "Mahn-kers") who held me when no one else could. They understood me and loved me no matter what, and locked tight the secrets no one but us knew. In *Until The Darkness Takes Us,* I talked a lot about how classical monsters like Dracula and Jekyll & Hyde became entities that I called upon to look after me, pulling them over me like a blanket. They would speak through me, and I through them, as I desperately sought self-preservation and a barrier to my pain. Through and after the real-life horrors I lived, they became how I interacted and survived – nothing was scarier than what I was facing down, and so what might have terrified other small children my age comforted me.

Very randomly in July of 2017, an idea came to me. I was playfully discussing my monsters and what names I would give some new ones as an adult (e. g., "A Very

Birdie Harry"), when the idea turned into something much more meaningful and a whole lot darker. Because publicly discussing what my Mahnkers did for me as a child was still fresh, there was a sudden dam that broke within me and, in the Notes app on my phone in the middle of lunch, the book *Many Mysterious Monsters* was born. In one single sitting, without pause or reflection, the words came spilling out, and there it was – a message to my younger self. In that book, I was able to give thanks and respect to my monsters, disarming their perceived scaries and providing children like my own a new perspective on all that monsters could be.

    I immediately knew I had to get this out into the world. Over the next several weeks, I pulled together my trusted team to help me bring every idea I had for this release to life. The book was beautifully illustrated: I gave each monster a task, an age, a personality, and a name. I showcased their likes and dislikes, even their hobbies, and they became completely lovable creatures. In the pre-sales, we did a few amazing child-sized monster dolls of one of the characters named "Little Brother." The book was, of course, released on Halloween that year. I am incredibly proud of all that it came to be: a gift to myself, my children, and everyone who has ever heard a bump in the night.

Beyond The Echoes In The Dark

On a sticky-hot August evening, I was settled in on our couch during the time of night when the house is finally still, the kids are in bed and I have a certain peace about me. My home has a hum at night - a soft and low beat within its wooden bones that is both calming and electric, an idiosyncrasy I blame on it being roughly a hundred years old. Often, that hum lulls me into a creative place, and that night I was almost aimlessly strumming a pattern on my guitar that kept pushing into my head when bits and pieces of word phrases began to formulate. I jumped up, ran over to my desk in the corner of the living room and frantically began working. The whole thing came out in about an hour, and I immediately sent it to Oise, whom I can always trust for complete honesty. He sprang into action right away, telling me "no more bullshit," and that now was the time to do my own thing. Oise encouraged me to keep going and pushed to have me move fast. He knew damn well that I would change my mind if given the chance, often teasing me that if left to my own devices, I'd have a band of gypsies on stage with me.

Once I got the feelings of "Echoes" out, I needed to get EVERYTHING out. It was almost like a geyser of pain and art after that. The songs just continued to write themselves, and I knew that to tell my full story, it ALL had to be told. I started talking about the songs I was writing publicly to hold myself accountable - if I gave up, everyone would know. In a move that likely annoyed the hell out of Oise who was frantically working to get me to the studio as fast as humanly possible, I would share small bits of the songs on social media to help me validate what I was doing; in turn motivating me to keep going. Other new songs bled out of me with the same speed and intensity as "Echoes," and

I felt like maybe I wanted to go back and reclaim some other pieces that I had released as part of past musical projects, too. I wanted to take them and do them the way I had envisioned them when they were still just sparks of ideas I couldn't carry out on my own. "Across Five Years," "Alone," "Quixote's Last Ride," - these songs were especially important to me to capture and make anew, and I love how each of them was reborn.

It took a lot of work to battle my loudest negative voices telling me in a hundred different ways that I was not good enough to do this thing. I was not good enough because I'm not making a difference, or because what I am doing doesn't matter to anyone but me. I am constantly afraid of opening myself up to others and it not being impactful to them - they can love it intensely or hate it with all the fires of hell, so long as their reaction isn't mediocre. Sometimes I beat the feelings of inadequacy, and sometimes I don't; but it's very important that I set myself up to be as successful as possible in the fight. I have chosen who I surround myself with more carefully these days, opting to be pushed by those who believe in me and can comfortably tell me to "shut up and do the damn thing" when my doubt takes over. I suppose the act of consistently putting my art out into the world when I struggle with this can be seen as a bit masochistic or even a form of self-harm; for me, it's a positive suffering and there is a certain charge in that. There's a part of me that needs that awkwardness and un-comfortability to show me that I'm doing the right thing. As much as I need the feeling of being vulnerable and exposed, I hate to disappoint people just the same.

One of the best ways for me to face down my fears is to move at the speed of light before I have time to overthink anything. Late September and early October of that year were insane. In the span of about four weeks, I released my first children's book, went to the studio to record my first solo album, filmed my first solo music video and played my first solo show. Absolutely bonkers.

About a month after I first wrote "Echoes," I was driving up to Asbury Park, NJ, to record at Little Eden Studios with Pete Steinkopf of The Bouncing Souls. This studio experience was wildly different than any I had ever been through before. It took me a bit to get used to the reality that I was the one running the show this time. I didn't have to wait for other people to show up and complete their parts so I could take my turn. There was a whole lot less creative input from others to consider as well. I remember saying to Pete something along the lines of "OK let's get started now" and him looking at me as if "yeah, just waiting on you to tell me what to do, dude - there's no one else here." I had such a great time working with Pete on the album. We got along very well, and I think Oise knew exactly what he was doing when he connected us for this part of the project. Pete really knew how to draw my best ideas and performances out of me. He had a very intuitive process of knowing when to speak up and when to let me lead and do my thing. It was the first time I ever got to have my name on an album as "producer" and every time I see it, the thought still fills me with pride. I can't believe we pulled it off so quickly – I was quite literally still writing songs just before we got started. Going into it, I wasn't sure what they would become because, at that point, most were still just raw and simple recordings on my phone.

I brought in an incredibly talented group of friends to lend their hands to a few songs in ways I could not. Elyse Nighthawk, who provided the intense and morose cello melodies, is someone who I had actually intended to be a part of The Casting Out at its inception. And while every song to which she brought her instrument on *Feral Hymns* was magic, being able to realize the song "Alone" with her string work as it was originally meant to be was an incredibly cathartic feeling. I invited Darren Deicide, another musician

I knew through shared social circles, to step in and provide a bit of his unique, devilish grit and swing to the song "Burn Away." And joining me for a few songs on that album was Becky Fontaine, a long-time friend of mine whose exquisite voice and harmony arrangements fit perfectly with both the mood and spirit of the story I was looking to tell.

Making the "Echoes" video was an incredibly cleansing experience. I had the idea to revisit the abandoned church in which Dan and I had portraits done a year prior for the *Until The Darkness Takes Us* album artwork, and make that space a canvas for what I had envisioned to somewhat complete the story. Thankfully, Bobby Bates was up to the task of bringing it to life. It was so hot the day we filmed. The church was full of dust and toppled pews and psalm books and sweat. The atmosphere was absolutely suffocating, and because it sits on the property of an abandoned boarding school, everything was eerily still. When we arrived, I carefully set the altar with photos of myself as a child, special mementos and hundreds of brightly colored flowers. I wanted it to have a bit of a Dia De Los Muertos vibe. We lit several dozen candles, and I took a breath and set my mind to the task. I haven't really done a lot of music videos, and I was pretty unsure of myself in front of the camera. So that day I just had to let go and trust my team to take my ideas and guide me into everything I had hoped for and more.

Being in that space and singing those words over and over again, take after take, was the catalyst for an enormous emotional shift. It was exhausting and freeing, as if I was saying goodbye and putting to rest feelings that had been holding me down and back. It was almost a memorial or funeral service to me. I had set out to entomb so many ghosts, so many scars and an infinite amount of fears. I wanted to release myself from all that weighed me down. If you look at that video carefully, you will notice a brief frame in which I am sitting in the pews, and there is a strange and very visible puff of air that comes out of my mouth. That is 100% real, and while we joke about it now that it was one of my demons leaving my body, I think it's a pretty symbolic coincidence. My team that day swears they saw it happen in front of the camera. While we can't decide on a logical reason for it (dust, heat, etc.,), I hold onto it as a symbolic moment of when something dark was freed from me. When we packed up at the end of the day, having spent six hours excommunicating myself through blood, sweat and tears, I left within those walls the black curtain from behind which I had been hiding. It was the day I decided to let go.

    Just four nights after filming the video, I played my first show. It was in a small club in downtown Baltimore that sat above a Chinese food restaurant and across the hall from a dance club. I have to laugh when I look back at those photos now – I played the whole set with my reading glasses on so I could see the lyrics on my iPad. I felt completely awkward, exposed and alone on that stage. Nerve-wracking would be an understatement. I could barely do more than pluck away at this guitar hiding my fear, hiding my bloated and sloppy body, and hiding my uncertainty. I had no idea what I was doing, but I knew that I had no other option. And I wasn't fucking giving up this time. The show went by in a blur, and afterwards, I felt absolutely horrible. I hadn't gotten out the feelings I intended in order to move myself forward, and I was extremely disappointed in myself. Beyond that, I was horrified that people had seen that train wreck go down. In all honesty, it went exactly as I expected it to go. I knew I wasn't ready to be on that stage, but I pushed ahead anyway because that is what I needed to do to get where I wanted to be.

    What was left of that year was spent in a dizzying rush of watching my first European tour as a solo artist sell out show after show during presale, getting my feet under me to put together a set list, practicing my songs, and spending time with family for the holidays. Everything was moving so fast, it was almost as if I had no time to be a mental disaster. But, because I am an overachiever, I somehow managed to make time for that, too.

There is a light where the darkness feels
no shame

There is a love that never has to fade

The Unlovable, Adored

I can't say for certain that others who have suffered some form of abuse find themselves inexplicably drawn to abusive situations throughout their post-traumatic life, but for me, that has absolutely been the case. Abuse is evil and purposeful, and no matter what form it takes – mental, physical, sexual or otherwise - it's meant to grind you into nothing until eventually that is where you become comfortable. Within abusive relationships over the years (both platonic and romantic), I began to find a twisted sense of belonging as I grew older. I sincerely believed that I did not deserve better, and I had learned to (more so been conditioned to) believe the lies that were consistently reinforced over the years. I remember being a very awkward young man around 12 or 13, right when girls became very, very interesting to me, and mustering up the courage to ask one out. It always played out like: "Hey, you wanna hang out some time? No? OK, yeah I guess that make sense. Have a nice day!" It was awful, and thinking back on those times now makes my skin crawl a bit. On the flip side, if someone *did* find something attractive, desirable or good in me, it kicked on a sort of defense mechanism where I felt if I *wasn't* being treated in an intensely negative way, something was "wrong" and I thought that meant they didn't care enough. Someone actually and honestly loving me made no sense in my brain, and I freely admit that that has been a life-theme for me.

When I moved from Pensacola, Florida, to North East Maryland, I had the opportunity to reinvent myself for that last year or so of high school. I didn't have to be a broken, weak and damaged boy. I could be a tough punk kid: outspoken, rough and giving no fucks about anyone. The more I wore that stand-offish, asshole persona, the more people gravitated toward me. I don't doubt a lot of it had to do with being the new kid in town, but girls started paying attention for once. If I got in trouble for refusing to stand for the pledge of allegiance, it made me interesting to them. To keep up the persona, when they would show interest, I played it off as though I didn't care, and that just made me even more appealing to them. The worse I acted, the more people validated it and I started to build my confidence on the backbone of that. It took me several years to reevaluate how I wanted to receive that power. I realized I had a certain duty to be better when more and more eyes looked to me as an ideal once boysetsfire started to gain some ground. I had to learn that not all attention is positive and beneficial for gaining self-love and self-confidence, and not all adoration is worthy of filling our empty hearts. Sometimes, all you're really doing is dousing yourself in gasoline and handing someone a book of matches, begging them not to strike one.

    As an adult, I found myself gravitating towards very specific styles of abuse which spoke directly to my trauma-born feelings of worthlessness. I ended up finding myself in some wildly toxic environments because of it. Verbal abuse. Humiliation. Manipulation. Physical abuse. Emotional de-programming. Time and again I would allow myself to be drawn in by people who rained these desecrations down upon me, and I would relentlessly forgive them until everything bottomed out. A lot of what I went through as an adult was very strategic and malicious - the more covert the act is, the more abusive it is, and yet, somehow, I could not keep myself away from it. In cycles of repetitive masochism, I would enable these people to hurt me over and over again, even when warning signs were lit up like marquees on Broadway. It was as if I could instinctively seek out the most narcissistic person in the room, and without pause, I would set my sights on winning that person's affection. Only now can I look back on that desperation for what it truly was: me trying to answer the "why" of my afflictions and convince myself that there could be love and perhaps even respect within abuse.

I went through a period of being an intentional victim – a sword I threw myself on in a desperate move to find answers, find validation and find a distraction from the noise in my head. It took me way too long to break free from those cycles and recognize that not only did I deserve better, but I could be better. By nature, narcissistic abusers seek to capture and destroy someone stronger than them for their own amusement and satisfaction in order to elevate themselves. I let too many of them get too close to doing just that. A trio of them, to be exact. Through those relationships, I have been toyed with, talked down to in circles until I no longer remembered what was real and what was the lie being fed to me, locked up, knocked down, taunted, hidden, made to feel more ashamed than I already did, made to feel guilty for things as simple as very normal reactions to stress, threatened, mercilessly teased, abandoned and broken. All in the name of love.

In a grand finale move, I ended up getting involved in a very long round of torture with someone who was a most deviously impressive and meticulous Gaslighter. Different than the woman I spoke of in *Until The Darkness Takes Us* who humiliated me in ways I still struggle to come to terms with, this one operated by methods that were much more psychologically damaging. Our multi-year "relationship" became so unhinged, I almost got addicted to feeling wrong. We would get into arguments where I would know with full certainty (armed with concrete proof of her transgressions) that I was correct about something she had said or done, but she would be SO convicted in her story and feigned such Oscar-worthy disbelief, that it made me extremely confused as to what reality even was. It was a constant batting of her eyes to distract me from the cut of her silver tongue. She would draw me into an argument, push me to manic hysteria, and then go completely dark, later reappearing as if nothing at all had happened. There would be a buildup of so many things that upset me, that they would stack on top of each other until I started forgetting what had started the argument. Each time she returned, it would be painfully apparent that none of my feelings were being heard, and no evil deed or word would be genuinely apologized for or met with any sort of emotional maturity. I felt constantly on edge.

The happier times were only reintroduced when I would push down all that hurt in an effort to try to let it go for the "greater good." (Although in retrospect, there wasn't much genuine happiness I felt in that time period with her. It became cyclical in that sense.) I think a part of me let her do so much lying to my face because if I called her out, it was her being caught, not her being honest. I became somewhat drawn to the negative energy because, for all its chaos, it took up a lot of brain space and provided a constant distraction from my core pain. Unfortunately, I believe she knew that and relished it. Everything she did perpetuated my feelings of low self-worth, and I spent many days and nights hysterical and out of my mind. With dizzying regularity, she would walk away from me and go back to a man (who had been in her life longer than I) who she told me time and again was terrible to her and who made her deeply unhappy. Every single time she did so, I was left wondering why someone claiming to love me was hurting me and why she was letting someone else "win" her love over me. The only answer my inner voices ever gave was that I wasn't deserving of love and happiness. It was all very cold, calculated and evil.

It is nearly impossible to explain the all-encompassing confusion I experienced during that time period. There are countless examples of maltreatment from those years, things to this day I am working to recognize and let go of. There were multiple occasions I felt pushed to the brink of insanity, attempting to carry on a normal life to the outside world, when inside I could think of nothing but an obsessive circle of "Why? Why don't you love me?". And there literally was no answer. There's never going to be an answer or closure given for abuse of any kind because, in the end, it was never about the victim, and it's tough to protect yourself from that kind of self-serving malice. And THAT is the hardest thing to come to terms with - it's just a thing that happened, and you can't get into the head of the person who is doing/did it. Reconciling that is incredibly difficult, and much like someone with a substance addiction, you generally don't stop going back to what is killing you until you hit rock fucking bottom. I would often walk or be pushed away from this relationship, promising the people who cared about me that I would stop letting her drag me through glass. A week or two would go by and I would be backsliding right into her madness. Every empty apology she made, every damsel in distress cry for attention led me right back to her, finding myself once again sweeping the fight to the side and swallowing my hurt deep into my belly.

    I can only assume that I kept going back because I believed that if I just did something more, she would love me in return. That if I was better and just showed her how much pain I could take; she would grow to love me. In reality, I believe she was incapable of doing so, and I was simply fighting a one-sided battle. Whatever piece of myself that I was looking for within that relationship was never going to be found, but I couldn't admit that to myself at the time. And I couldn't admit to myself that I had made a mistake in allowing myself to lay my weapons at the feet of someone who would only take them into her hands and use them against me. It took me years to break that cycle, feeling complete panic every time I tried to break it off. Once a little distance got between us, I would spiral out of control, wondering if my sorrow in missing her meant I made a mistake in leaving. It was a lot like detoxing from drugs or alcohol, and I would often give up every time the tremors began. Each time we split up, there would be bouts of intense agony as I caved in on myself, trying to cool a burning in my stomach while wrestling with which parts of my memories were real and if things were as bad as I interpreted them.

As I've said before when referring to my domestic disparagements: *"I was not a victim of abuse, but a co-conspirator in the demise of my self-worth."* Every time I put myself through this, it would directly correlate with my intense quest for control. For answers. If I could just push these experiences of self-abuse through the hands and lips of others, perhaps I could rationalize or understand the purpose of my afflictions. There's a cycle of pain and self-medication here. I was trying to mend wounds from the sexual abuse by solving some unsolvable puzzle. I will *never* know why my childhood abusers tormented me in darkened prayer rooms. But if I could maybe find an answer within these horrible experiments in searching for what love meant now, perhaps I would at least find peace. I was willing to excuse far too many red flags because I desperately sought a feeling of safety - a life vest to embrace me through the tsunami of heartache. In reality, all I was really doing was strapping pretty rocks to my chest. I felt alone and ashamed, believing that love was only real if it scarred me. I was willing to sacrifice my sanity and my soul if it just meant I could be whole, never realizing that I already was.

It took a lot of work, a lot of failure, and a lot of time and distance for me to recognize that my struggle to find "reality" was a direct symptom of the gaslighting itself. I eventually, albeit painfully, got to a better place. This was in no small part due to me systematically sharing my story with people I trusted who (perhaps not patiently and not without heartache of their own) helped me dissect and reflect. Being open and honest about my experience in real-time held me accountable while I worked to eliminate the subconscious need to find approval and self-worth within the relationship. I committed to myself that I would pull myself out of this thing and that I would find who I was *without* her, even in the times the memory of her was still renting space in my head. Each time we split up I got a little stronger, and I know that likely sounds a bit insane considering, but it was a process. I knew that I just had to keep pushing forward - even when I fell - because as long as she was around, I wouldn't find the self-love I was seeking.

The wildly ironic part of these cyclical times of my life was that I was so wrapped in toxic webs, I was ignoring that I was hurting the people who truly and effortlessly loved me and were trying to teach me to love myself. I know you aren't technically supposed to find self-worth and a platform for loving yourself within others, but maybe - just *maybe* - it is possible to be loved so rightly and purely that we begin to love ourselves as a reflection of what we are receiving. We begin to see ourselves as others do, especially those who embrace and protect the parts of us we are least likely to *want* to love. Some of the most impactful people in my life have loved me assertively and consistently by reminding me often that: "You're wrong, but I'm not going anywhere" and "I'm not leaving, but I'm also not going to stop telling you when you are wrong." What I have learned from them is that love is firm and constant, but it does not enable. It does not encourage or perpetuate self-destructive behaviors or thought patterns. It does not turn a blind eye. It builds us up instead of tearing us down. It is a freely and happily made decision by each half of the whole to love and be loved in return.

I recognize that it can be intense and exhausting and painful and terrifying to care about someone like me who is struggling to break free from an abusive past (or present), or who is working through some trauma, a dark period of depression, anxiety, panic, or a seemingly endless string of bad days. Just don't give up on us. We know we are a lot of work, but we appreciate those willing to stay and fight alongside us. You don't have to solve our problems for us, but it is incredibly valuable and important when you are open to just sit and listen. For me, conversations that left me feeling most supported were approached in a manner of "I can't fix this for you, but I will walk through your pain with you." If I can offer you any advice on how to guide a similar conversation, let it be this:

- Ask us questions - "How does that make you feel?" and "How can I help?" (Often the answer will be "you can't," but know that listening is enough.)
- Know when to stop pushing and allow us to decompress. We will return to the conversation when we are ready.
- Don't give advice unless asked or given permission.
- Just be there. That's it.

 I chose to speak of all of this now to give you some deeper insight into who I am, where I've been and what my battle has been behind the stage lights. What happened to me as a child set in motion decades of aftermath that affected me in many, many ways. A lot of the pieces from my first two solo albums, and the EP between them, document my journey of learning to find self-love by living through the shitty experiences that showed me what love was NOT. These songs walk through the feelings themselves as I dug up all that I buried in an effort to finally and firmly cleanse myself. They are a play-by-play of my process of becoming comfortable in my heart and mind, and working towards really, truly believing that I deserve all the good things life has to offer. I did not come this far to just come this far. Every single day I am learning to love myself and be loved in return, and hopefully being open about my journey will help others on theirs.

There are people close to me who have suffered through similar experiences. Their stories are unique to mine, but they're left with damage much the same – people held captive by spouses in their closets overnight; people pushed into walls while holding their newborns; people sexually exploited, coerced or molested; people who were tortured and verbally beaten down. People who've been told to kill themselves and have replayed that so many times in their head, the idea seems reasonable. Many of them afraid to speak their stories out loud. I suppose, aside from the rightfully selfish motivation of needing to heal, part of me feels a certain purpose or responsibility to use my voice to bring to light some of these things millions go through every day. If you are struggling to find the strength to walk away from something that deep down you know is doing more harm than good, please know that the only way out is jumping with both feet. You will never get better unless you commit to severing the ties completely; at least until you have fully taken your strength and power back. Time and distance will, eventually, build you back up. And understand that a part of healing is allowing yourself to be broken and knowing that it's OK to feel lost.

You are not alone. We are NOT alone. **It wasn't our fault.**

Pot. Kettle. Black

Certainly there have been relationships (and friendships) in my life that were very good, pretty normal and mostly healthy, but as the human experience goes, we tend to learn more lessons from the hard fails than the times we felt happy and safe. It's sad, but true. And for the purpose of this book, it is more important for me to dig into those hard falls and bring their lessons out not only for myself, but anyone else who might benefit or need perspective.

In all honesty, there was a time where I, too, was an absolute drunken trash-monster. What I intended to be my "fun" phase of life, doing as I pleased and answering to no one, ended up becoming an absolute train wreck. I think a lot of people who were around during the time of The Casting Out never really saw what was happening behind the scenes. While I am not proud of who I was, how I coped, or how I treated others, it is a real part of my story and I am unafraid to own it. Almost no one I lashed out at during that time of my life deserved it. I completely embarrassed not only myself in those times, but people very dear to me. I would drink and drink until that little demon in my mind started rubbing his hands together like a hungry Hyde to my Jekyll, and I'd immediately and belligerently pick a fight with whoever was closest that I felt confident would not fight back. It was utterly gross behavior.

Because I was in such an inebriated state during those years, my recollections of those times were (perhaps somewhat selectively) a bit clouded. I decided to turn to someone who could best share the impact my behavior had on those around me so that I could write about it honestly for the purpose of the book and Jesus Christ, I ended up getting more insight than I anticipated. Oise Ronsberger has been by my side (both personally and professionally) for as long as I can remember, and he has put up with a lot of shit from me. So much so, that it's probably fair to say that I have often been undeserving of his unwavering support. Together, we were able to lay out a lot of the timeline through my descent, which honestly left me feeling pretty ashamed of myself, but gave me incredible outside perspective.

After what I had been through with Matt in boysetsfire, a partnership that was just completely unhealthy in every single way, and the subsequent break for the band, I decided that I would set out to do my own thing and that I would never again let anyone tell me what to do. After spending years being controlled by his aluminum fist, I was done. I would never again answer to someone else while sacrificing my integrity, my vision, my voice and my mental health. That said, I went SO far in the other direction, I began like acting out like a 15-year-old in a "dad's gone, and I can do what I want" manner. Anyone who had an opinion, told me no or asked me to see things in a different way, I took as trying to control me. And I was out to fight anything and anyone I perceived as an authority figure. It was arrogant, defiant and sloppy, and, although I do not *completely* regret the sentiment, I regret that I hurt others in the process.

Once I got The Casting Out up and running, we headed out to Europe for our very first tour, and somehow, amazingly, played to 500 - 600 people a night; it was an incredible experience. In the absence of boysetsfire, I think many people were very interested in hearing what I was doing, and they were all-in on supporting this adventure. Our sound was very upbeat and it provided an energetic live show that fans were drawn to. Behind the scenes, though, we were just complete drunken idiots. For example, we very pretentiously put champagne on our rider that tour, popping the bottles in grand, idiotic gestures. One night when the cork shot out, it broke the stage monitors. When the house got upset with us (rightly so), I laughed and told them off, challenging them to tell me, "Nathan Fucking Gray," that I was in the wrong. I stood up to everyone in those days, refusing to listen to reason, even if being told "no" was for a completely *rational* reason and in my best interest, which, to be honest, it most often was.

On another occasion, Oise had a friend (our tour manager for that run of shows actually) backstage, and I threw a bottle of Jack Daniels at the guy, laughingly watching it shatter at his feet. When he got upset that the shards had hit his leg, I berated him for being weak. I'm fairly certain I destroyed the dressing room that night as well. I was just completely unbearable and no one knew how to handle me in those days. I got progressively worse as time went on, becoming the Matt I hated – wild, irrational and unpredictable.

There were many instances in which I even acted like a complete asshole to people for the sole purpose of getting attention. I walked around like a version of myself in high school, but on steroids. Mean, angry and drunk, I didn't much care about anything or anyone – all that mattered was that I was the life of the party when my demons came out to play.

For many, many years prior to this debaucherous time of my life, I walked around with an uncomfortable and unexplainable feeling fogging the back of my conscience. Like a bathroom mirror after a hot shower, I could make out shapes of memories, but not enough to see exactly what they were. I just knew they were something that horrified me. No doubt in an effort to protect myself from them, I shut down, pushing back the demons who snapped and snarled on their leashes as I tightened their collars, never wanting to wipe that mirror clean to see myself on the other side. As a child, I locked away the reality of my abuse, not sure what exactly I had experienced, knowing only that it was dark and very, very wrong. I continued to push the memories off until I thought they were gone, just wanting to be rid of them altogether. As I grew older, the more I struggled to keep those memories docile, the more the darkness itself became an untamable beast, gradually becoming more and more rabid until there was a magnificent snapping of everything that held me together, and all that I had been so diligent to keep at bay came flooding in. I guess I couldn't stay happily ignorant forever.

Around the time I was working to put The Casting Out together, the reality of my sexual abuse began to show itself to me as a rapid-fire replay of many, many unwelcome memories, and I completely lost control. I dealt with it wasted and unemployed with no ambition or direction, choosing instead to spend my time playing video games. (Remember a few chapters ago when I told you about the day I wanted to put a gun in my mouth? Yeah. Same time of life.) I didn't really talk about what I was going through to those around me who likely could've helped. To be honest, if they *would've* asked why I was acting out so badly, I'd have just freaked out on them anyway. I was in absolutely no state of mind to receive kindness and understanding. No state of mind to put a plan together for healing. I just wanted to get drunk, have fun and forget how broken I felt. As Oise so perfectly stated, it was "the saddest 'fun' I had ever seen." While I certainly WANTED to relax and have a good time, I was in no mental place to understand what healthy fun was in those days. Even when I was piss-drunk, I wasn't happy and I definitely wasn't enjoying myself.

I sincerely want to punch myself in the face when I think back to who I was during that time. The only energy I spent was on getting that band rolling, and, ironically, I myself was the one that made it implode. I was pushing my bandmates and friends way too hard at all the wrong times, making bad decisions and listening to no one who had my best interests in mind. My wild intensity and "give-no-fucks" attitude exhausted all of them, and rightly so.

    I felt like a caged animal for the next several years, snarling and crouched over my trauma, trying to keep it from being seen. People who got too close to peering into me would be shoved off immediately. Once I bore witness to what had happened to me, I walked around utterly paranoid, like someone stoned who thinks everyone they pass on the street knows their deep, dark secret. My entire body and soul hurt from being in 24/7 fight-or-flight mode, ready to run if I felt looked into too deeply or too long. In what I can now assume was in an effort to protect myself, I just began lashing out and throwing tantrums like a bratty kid - selfish and rude. I suppose I was somewhat stunted in my trauma-state, and I had this angry inner-child who was acting out in very adult ways.

    Gradually, that confident façade I took on in my teenage years became more aggressive and mean. It was a mask I wore through the writing and release of *While a Nation Sleeps*, and through the period of I AM HERESY where I was deepest within my savage anger. Everything came to a head not long before *Until The Darkness Takes Us* came out. I would often lock myself into arguments on Facebook for days in those final months of my vicious phase. I always believed I was doing the "right" thing for whatever cause I decided to take up, but I never went about it in the right way. I just drew a proverbial line in the sand and took on religion, politics, people who rubbed me wrong, magazines which I felt had slighted me, and anyone who dared disagree with me on ANY subject at all, never giving pause to consider what personal or professional relationships I might be ruining in the process. It was just an overall horrible time of life, and every bit of it was exacerbated by my own actions. (Please note: In the last year, I actually felt myself slipping into this pattern during an emotionally low period, this time using Twitter as a platform/catalyst for my aggression. Thankfully,

I was able to recognize the behavior, call myself out on it and deactivate my account before it got out of hand again. It's important for me to share that to keep myself accountable and to show that the work and growth truly is constant.)

Looking back, it is obvious to me that in forcing myself to skip the steps in processing my grief, I created within myself an absolute fucking monster. Not the endearing kind, like those wonderful childhood protectors of mine, but a spiteful, vengeful, angry, selfish monster. Spinning out of control, I had no plan of attack to face down my demons, no hope for *ever* getting better and no motivation to even try to function within my trauma. When I fell, it would last days, weeks, even, and I became comfortable having that horrible attitude as a defense mechanism. A false front. My security blanket. I never saw myself healing, and essentially just gave up – dead set on taking the world down with me.

It has taken some very diligent self-awareness and reconciliation to pull myself out of that phase. None of this is meant to excuse my behavior, only to provide a backstory to it. I am 100% accountable for my actions and for how I treated the world around me. I can't take back this phase of my life, but I *can* (and do) work my ass off to be better. And I think what I'd like people to get from this chapter most is that we should never let our past dictate how we treat others in our present. If we all walk around projecting our pain onto the world around us, the world itself is destined to fail. It's human to struggle and it's human to have bad days, but it's absolutely NOT acceptable to drag the rest of the world down with you in your misery. I fucked up, I am still learning from it, and if you happen to be someone who was undeservingly at the receiving end of my wrath, this is me, sincerely apologizing to you.

Black out, wake up, start swinging, face the pain

Failures come and go but that's OK

:Insert Chumbawamba Lyrics Here:

I often get messages asking me for advice, especially now as my journey has taken me down a more positive road filled with both mental and physical benefits. And while I try to answer each one, the reality is that I'm figuring this life out as I go, too, and what works for me may not work for you. If nothing else, I hope that people can learn a little from my mistakes, indiscretions, implosions and general shithead behaviors. This is not a self-help book, and I am no Guru. Rather than tell you what will work for you, I simply share what my personal journey has looked like. Maybe you'll find some inspiration; maybe you'll decide that I am full of shit. Either way, this is my truth, and I live it despite your determinations.

The first piece of comfort I can offer is that all paths we take are "for now," and we can stop and course-correct at any time. No matter how it may feel, you are never stuck eternally within a time, place or emotion. The second is that You. Are. Going. To. Fail. You will fail over and over again. Glamorously and disastrously. You will taste defeat. You will (more than a few times) give up and cry for mercy. What I want for you is that you learn to see the beauty in your failures and the growth in your defeat. I fully admit that my ideology was a bit off when it came to the idea of/acceptance of failure. I'm not saying I was kicking dirt in the faces of people around me when they fell; I'm saying that for me, I based my successes and failures on some very unrealistic and dangerous expectations. I was very success driven and, opposed to making an effort to see the journey itself as the thing to be proud of, I needed "accomplishments" or I would beat myself up over the failures in order to be better next time around. This applied to my music, my relationships, my work, my role as a father, my duty as a leader, you name it.

I was falling so hard after my failures that it was getting in the way of my actual progress. What's worse is I was the one getting in my own way. I know MANY driven individuals who do this to themselves over and over again. We get so caught up in the ideal we have built in our heads that we actually slow ourselves down from getting to the goal. What I had to start telling myself was to just get the fuck back up and try again. It became a little easier to do when I could stop myself from falling into the pit of despair by asking myself two questions:

1) What did I learn about myself in that failure?
2) How can I be better next time?

Try it! Hell, start writing down your answers every time you find yourself face down in the dirt. Then in a year, go back to that and see what progress you've made. I can bet your perception of "failure" will change, too.

I've recently tried to be much more cognizant of what I share and don't share on social media. The internet is a dangerous place these days; no longer is it a place to listen and a place to connect and share ideas. It has degenerated into a place where we see all the extremes and none of the balance as millions work to romanticize the impossible. A place where people you've never even passed in the street will set out to shit on everything you care about or stand for. I truly believe that it's on all of us to play a part in calling attention to such behavior, combating it with mindful respect and encouragement of vulnerable realness. I am working to share my good AND bad days with people and hope that it inspires others to do the same. None of us are perfect. None of us. So let's normalize the normal, shall we? I can promise you that you sharing your dark days with the same gusto with which you share your happiest moments will create a ripple effect in your social circles to do the same. I've seen it happen. Further, and I know this is a wild concept, but if social media makes you not feel good about yourself, you can (and maybe should) just delete your profiles. If it doesn't make you feel good, you literally don't have to do it. Same with friends, family, addictions or anything of the sort – **you are not (and should not be) a martyr for your mental health.**

I know a lot of people are wondering if I have ever been to professional therapy, and the answer is "no." That's not to say I won't, but if I do, it will be on my own terms, and in my own time. I recognize that seeing a therapist has significant value and can be incredible helpful for many, but I truly believe that traditional therapy is not the only avenue for growth and healing – that peace can come from emotional self-work in many forms. For me, it has been beneficial to share and seek understanding from people I trust, such as very close friends and family, who often hold a symbolic mirror to help me see myself as they do. Good or bad, that small act ignites necessary self-reflection, where I begin to do my own healing work. I encourage everyone to start close to home, but if you do not have a trusted friend or family member, then perhaps a professional is the route for you. Perhaps even if you have more friends and family than you know what to *do* with, a professional therapist is still the route for you. I know that many people fear burdening or scaring those they care about with their feelings, and the only safe way for them to express themselves fully is in a transactional, professional relationship as opposed to an emotional one. I will (and have) always support the healthiest, safest option for whoever it is in need of help - you have to follow your own instincts, nuances and neuroses when it comes to tapping into your soul. I know many of you are, like me, wondering: "How can I get help without freaking out the part of me that I am protecting?" I definitely can't answer that for you, but I know that whatever form of healing you choose should feel safe, or it becomes more harmful than helpful. Sometimes Band-Aids® are important - they really are meant to protect you from open wounds. Not everyone understands that, and although these protective actions can sometimes be seen as self-harming from the outside (e.g., closing yourself off from others), when you examine what people use as protection, you'll learn a lot about who they are. As for me, no one is meant to know my trauma the way I do, because only I know how to handle and care for it in the way that both it and I need. At least for now.

    I recognize that I am extremely lucky to have an outlet to channel my emotions into; I shudder to think how swallowed up I would be if I didn't have my music and my time on stage (or even this book, and the one before!) to work through my heart's achings. I know there are many of you out there who do not have this particular avenue of catharsis, and so you are walking through life carrying your secrets like cannon balls in your stomachs. I promise you that holding in whatever hurts you is making you sicker. If you are uncomfortable talking to someone (either familiar *or* professional), I am begging you to find something safe you can pour your aching into. If you are looking for an outlet and feeling at a loss, I want you to try something for me – go to the store and pick up a new notebook. It can be as plain or as fancy as you like. Then, when the moment feels right, pick up a pen and write out all the things you are afraid to speak aloud. They don't have to be poetic, properly punctuated or even make sense. Put down all of your most intense feelings, your deepest secrets, the things you fear and are afraid to be known. It can even be just stream of consciousness ramblings. There will be no one to judge or mock or question what you write. No one to hurt. No one to worry. Just put the words down and get them out of your lungs so you can breathe. Write your goals or your biggest dreams – anything you want to document your growth through. Don't stop writing when you are overwhelmed with emotion, no matter what feelings the process drags up. Stop when the work feels done for the moment - a time only you can call. When you find a bit of peace, put the notebook away in a safe place and know that your secrets are now protected somewhere outside of yourself. You will then be free to move through life a little lighter. When you are *really* ready to let those feelings go, burn the fucking notebook. Make it a purposeful, private event - a ritual of letting go. When I finished writing *Until The Darkness Takes Us*, I burned six notebooks, a pile of paper, some napkins and a few old receipts in my backyard one chilly November evening. It was a simple, but very final, statement to myself to watch my notes go up in flames. As I work through *Light & Love*, I am already looking forward to that gesture again, eager to watch all my pain transform to ash as I say goodbye.

    I think it's probably fairly obvious that even as I make strides forward, I fall back a step every now and again. It's become incredibly important to me to be honest and real about the times I fall because I think a lot of us get stuck on the idea that failure is both final and shameful. It feels as if we have lost some great race and everyone around us has effortlessly crossed the finish line. Believe me when I tell you that it is OK to not be OK, though. Failure IS an option, and we must learn to embrace it as a part of the normal human experience. Failure is not our enemy; it can be a learning tool if we can just teach ourselves to see it as such. We open ourselves to learn so much about who we are each time we rise from a fall, especially when we're gentle enough with ourselves to know that failure will, most assuredly, come again. Allow room for it. Forgive yourself for it. Find a tiny scrap of hope, even if it comes as a fleeting five-second smile from a stranger on a day when the other 86,395 seconds of those 24 hours are full of pain. Hold onto it fiercely…that scrap is enough to carry you into another morning on this Earth, I promise. And god dammit, don't be afraid to speak up and ask for help when you need it, in whatever way is most comfortable for you.

Through some decidedly clumsy trial and error, I have learned to work through the best way for me to get help when I need it most. I have finally gotten myself to a place where I can vocalize "I am in distress right now" as I am hanging off a cliff. I admit, though, it took a bit of work for both myself and my loved ones to understand that in those times, I am quite unable to actually tell others HOW specifically to help me. Many people are great at asking for what they need - I am not, and I am grateful for those closest to me who understand that my care must be somewhat intuitive. People like me are best helped by those who pay attention to the unspoken scars, triggers and intricacies. Sometimes we just need to be saved from ourselves.

All that said, now that I have committed myself to facing down and working through my own traumatic experiences, I have noticed (as have those closest to me) that it has honestly become easier for me to recover from or bounce back from my bad days/weeks. They are not non-existent of course, as there are still some very painful and agonizingly cyclical times of heartache, but it takes more intense situations for me to become triggered back into uncomfortable places these days. And when I am in one, I am able to recognize where I am at and tell myself: "You'll get through this. This feeling will end. At some point it will probably return, and that's nothing we can't handle." Hilariously, I think I often do my greatest, most productive work in the first hours and days after bouncing back from a low point – maybe it's a bit maniacal, I don't know. What I DO know is that my best writing, my best composing and my most creative work on re-modeling the house is done in those time of recovery.

My general attitude and outlook on life are much more positive now. I feel a complete 180-degree flip from where I was even just a year ago. I feel lighter; physically I feel the darkness lifting off, and the world around me seems so much more colorful. No one could have convinced me in the past that the life I am creating in my heart now would be possible, but here the fuck I am – doing it with a smile.

My Family, My Tribe

If ever a constant I have had, my family is one that has been invaluable; they are humbling, persistent, and aggressively loving without fail. They have been my impetus and inspiration to be better, there with me when I've needed consistency and peace most. Our home is our fortress and our castle, a place we have created with warmth and color, and within it there is safety like no other. Through even my darkest days, my family members have helped me find the energy to keep going simply by being themselves. They are my purpose and my hope, and they are all I know of faith and love.

I would say I fall somewhere between hyper-vigilant father and student of my children's love, which is the purest thing that I have ever known because it comes with full honesty and unquestioning devotion. Children are adorably selfish, not caring one bit that you're having a dark day; one in which the thought of getting out of bed or attempting to be in public seems like the most difficult thing on the planet to do. They don't care that you are heads-down, writing a new song or practicing your set in the dining room -- "Dad, push me on the swing. I want to go to the park. Can we get ice cream? I want meatballs. Can you build a tower with me? Can I borrow your amp for practice? Let's watch Avengers. Watch this video. I want to paint. Can you come over and help fix my car? Help me put three princess dresses and my brother's underwear on at the same time, RIGHT NOW." There is absolutely no dull moment, and I am grateful for all three of them, each of whom amusingly seems to carry a personality that reflects one of my own.

I've learned a lot of patience from my family, and I imagine I still have much left to learn as Simon, Aleksander and Sophia continue to grow older. For my tiny but mighty

Sophie, I've decided to start the work of intentional parenting now, preparing myself to not be the sort of guy who assumes his daughter is his property, which is this disturbing act that has somehow become socially acceptable. Chad has always been very good at empowering autonomy with his daughters (which I have always admired) and I have been cognizant that I offer Sophie the same, even in this early place of her life. I want her to grow up knowing that she is an individual and deserves respect and an equal playing field. For instance, Aleks doesn't get to do whatever he wants while I shield her from everything under the sun, being overprotective simply because she is female. That kind of approach is wildly damaging to not only his self-worth, but hers – they must have equal opportunities AND boundaries.

    I know the world is not exactly set up for her to easily thrive within, however. She will have to work her ass off for all that she desires, and it hurts my heart that she will have to ask: "Can I make the same amount of money as my male coworkers? Can I not worry that the government is going to take away my right to do as I please with my body? Can my voice be heard without being called a bitch for asserting myself? Can I walk alone at night and feel safe?" When the world is telling her how pretty, cute and beautiful she is, I hope to remind her that she is also strong, brave, kind, intelligent and independent. I hope to instill in her that THESE are the qualities that define her. When the world asks for hugs and kisses, I will remind her that it is her choice whether or not to oblige, and that she is 100% allowed to refuse. I hope to teach her that she does not owe anyone affection - not even me. I will always be here to hold her hand, but not too tight. I promise to be loving, but not controlling. I want to remind her that she is special, precious and loved beyond compare, but that I recognize that I do not own her and she is not a possession. She is a gift to care for until she is able to make her own decisions, be they good or bad. Above all, I hope to show her that she is worthy of respect and that with hard work and an open heart, she will conquer all that stands in her way. I will work to help empower her to be the strong, vibrant, and independent spirit she needs to be to survive this world. And I will open myself to be taught by, helped by, and cared for by her in return. We are meant to earn our children's love. We are not owed it, and how lucky we are when they come to gift it to us.

Somehow, my first-born is 25. Time has absolutely slipped away, and I look at Simon now, seeing the incredible man he has become, and feel such an intense pride in how hard he has fought to be where he is. It is definitely surreal to see him taking on such worldly responsibilities, killing it at work, (earning one promotion after another,) and even playing music again. I can't help remembering the days of our trips to the park to play on jungle gyms, or when he traveled to Europe with me as a teen to roadie for The Casting Out, and how amazing it was to share the stage with him in I AM HERESY. I admit that while watching him go through his own heartaches in life, I had to learn the hard way to stop reacting and making it about me and how I felt. I had to learn to stop trying to take his pain and suffering from him, and stop channeling it into my own anger, guilt and fear. I simply had to stop and just love him where he was at. Watching him thrive has been one of my greatest joys in life. Seeing him sitting at the dinner table at Thanksgiving this past year, cheerfully carrying on conversations with friends and family, his eyes bright and happy, face warm and smiling ear to ear, gives me hope that he will continue to create the life that was meant for him as he moves through it.

Aleksander, my amazing middle child, is a complete and unapologetic free spirit – he knows no strangers and came into this world looking as if he had all the answers. He is more comfortable in his own skin than I can ever recall being, even before my life experiences led me to feel shame about my body. I am quite honestly relieved at his autonomy because he has thankfully retained his innocence instead of me unintentionally begrudging him my own shame. I work hard to not transfer my brand of insanity to my family, encouraging each of them to be fearless, try new things and find comfort in their skin. I do my best to keep my more obsessive and off-beat behaviors in check, choosing to tuck them away or put on a brave face, meticulous to not let my more irrational fears fly out of my mouth. I know that children learn more from what we DO than what we say; so when I swallow back the panic in my throat over some very normal, very innocent and child-like thing that might have triggered something less than cheerful, I do it with them in mind, always. I would never forgive myself if I transferred my trauma onto them. I do carry a lot of guilt over how I showed up in the first years of all three of my children's lives though, and I admit that I wasn't always as present as I could have been, often succumbing to my own mood swings and toxic influences when I should have been more focused on my family. I am grateful that I had the opportunity to see myself clearly and course-correct that sort of behavior sooner rather than later.

    I will be the first to admit that I am an emotional creature, a revelation that would come as no surprise to anyone. I have always been free with my emotions, and I don't apologize for that. I feel things very deeply and am unashamedly sensitive to the world and the suffering it carries within it. If I am moved, I don't hold back - crying if need be and speaking my mind and heart when I am called to do so. Having that freedom has helped me get through a lot, and I realize that not every man (or woman) has been forged in the same way. My parents never made me feel self-conscious about my emotions the way I know some do. "Toughen up" or "Stop being such a sissy" or "Quit acting like a little girl" was never a way my mother or father would've spoken to me (or anyone else). I sincerely believe that it is stronger to cry when moved to do so and that showing emotion is a sign of great strength, not weakness. If there is anything at all I teach my sons in this life, I hope that it is that they understand they are welcome to be as free with their emotions as they feel comfortable.

    The idea of toxic masculinity is wildly dangerous, perhaps now more than ever, and I work hard to ensure that I don't feed any of those notions at home or in the world around me. It's the responsibility of all of us to help fix what is broken in society, and unlearning is Step One. Instilling that freedom in our children is Step Two. When I say "toxic masculinity," I think many of us (admittedly, myself included at one time), immediately picture a thick-necked, ignorant man in a tight Ed Hardy t-shirt with huge biceps, reeking of cheap cologne and trolling the internet, picking fights in comment sections and dropping unwanted nudes in the inboxes of females he's never even met. But I bet almost none of you picture a time when a male friend said "suck it up" when you (a male yourself) were hurting. Recognize that this is still toxic masculinity. Ironically, most of us men tend to only tell the other men in our lives that we love them when we are intoxicated. You know what I mean – the "I love you, man" conversation happening at 3 a.m. as you stumble out of a bar. We haven't been doing a great job of creating spaces for ourselves and the others in our lives to be vulnerable and have very normal emotions. Many of us grew up brushing off our problems out of fear of ridicule or being seen as weak instead of asking for the help we need or sharing when we are in a dark place. *Gentlemen, we are responsible for creating the space for each other to be human.* So let's hold each other accountable and start doing a better job at doing just that.

    I have noticed an inverse as a result of toxic masculinity: women still face the ideal that they smile, be "pretty," stay silent and be adaptable. Be polite. Never provoke (unless doing so sexually, of course). Don't get drunk. Do have children. They are met with eye-rolls when they show emotion. They are deemed aggressive when they express frustration. You are expected to leave your rights to the boys in ties, shave your legs and get out of the boardroom. When I look at my tiny, beautiful daughter, I have to wonder if these are battles she will be fighting for herself as she enters adulthood. Her autonomy and empowerment is not a gift her mother and I can give her, but one that she must stand and take on her own. I hope like hell she won't be expected to pry it from grubby hands.

My wife, Katie, has also taught me a lot about parenthood. She has absolutely stepped into her role as the matriarch of our family with grace and enthusiasm. I know she constantly worries about being a good mother, and I think that's what makes her great at it. She wants to be the best she can for them; to spend as much time as possible with them. She works extremely hard to give them the experiences they deserve in all aspects of life. She will be the first one to say hello to other children on the playground or at a party, and she's the first to get on the floor and play with them. I think a lot of adults somewhat overlook children or even look down on them as nuisances, but Katie effortlessly gives them her energy and attention. Her approach to parenting our own children is very pure and empowers them beautifully. I used to be really bad about letting them learn how to do things on their own, like tying shoes or putting on their own pants or shirts. I would get impatient and end up saying, "Let me just do it for you." She was always right there to remind me that I need to back off a little and give them space to figure things out for themselves.

Apart from all of the other wonderful things she does for our family, she takes on a lot when I am on the road, allowing me to live out my purpose in my music with the knowledge that all is well back home. My family takes my absence in stride when I am on tour, and through the magic of technology, we can FaceTime every night after my shows to say hello and goodnight. Despite the fact that when I am away from home I am living out my dream, being away from them is incredibly tough. It is both grounding and regenerating to be able to see their beautiful faces each day, even a continent or two away. I know it's never easy, but Katie has been a wonderful partner in this life and I am grateful for her. Her love, humor, ability to keep me grounded, and her unwavering support have been more than I could have ever hoped for.

I know that when it comes to the matter of family, I am beyond lucky. My support system is beautiful, vast and unwavering. I recognize that many others are not so lucky, and I can't imagine how difficult it must be to navigate this world with a family that is either absent or unsupportive. I would like to offer one thing for those of you struggling to feel at home – family is more than just who you were born "belonging" to - you are not obligated to continue forging relationships with blood relatives who don't lift you up. Certainly it can be said that every family has its struggles - we ALL have the occasional tiff over a holiday dinner. But when the scales tip towards dysfunction, know that you have the right to let go or to create your *own* ideal of family, building your tree with whatever branches and roots make you feel safe and loved. I have certainly adopted family members along the way who were chosen by circumstance rather than beholden to me by blood, and I am grateful for each and every person I hold dear, no matter how they found their way into my life.

Family First. Always.

Prepare for war don't let them under your skin

Remember where you've come from where you've been

And rose again to fight another day

And fall again to never be the same

FERAL HYMNS

When I was 12 years old, I wrote three albums. I mean…at the time, I only had the musical capacity to put the lyrics *themselves* down, but I carried the notes very vividly in my head. I made little paper LP sleeves by folding up lined notebook paper and stapling them into miniature pockets, and then I carefully wrote out the lyrics and slipped them into the sleeves. It was the 80's and I remember that one of the albums was very futuristic and admittedly ripped off Rick Springfield. I'm sure there was an overuse of the word "baby," as my verbal prowess was not yet fully realized. Not my most prolific work, but I would still grab my mom's tennis racket to use as a guitar and play to my reflection in our sliding glass door as if I were in a stadium rocking out for thousands of adoring fans. In January of 2018 (approximately 34 years later!) I released my first truly, honestly, absolutely solo album, *Feral Hymns*. And as chaotic as the year previous was, this year was much calmer and more purposeful - by my standards, anyway. There was an incredible amount of growth that occurred in the year that album came out, and I can say with certainty that it was one of my most significant years to date. Growth + Intention = Results. And all roads led me right here.

Just weeks after the album came out, I made my way to Europe for boysetsfire's second Family First Festival and, immediately after, jumped right into my first solo tour. What an incredible difference between those two experiences! As boysetsfire, we couldn't wait to try our hand at throwing another Family First Festival. The first one went off beyond our wildest dreams, and the possibility of being able to repeat that success was a huge step for us. Something that sticks out to me as one of the most special moments of that show ended up being something that we weren't even sure was going to work to begin with. Oise had this idea of building a small, nondescript stage in the middle of the audience, something people would overlook during the show itself. When we got to "Misery Index" in the set list, Chad and I walked up this pathway we had laid out that would take us through the crowd and sort of popped up on that small stage to begin the song. Just the two of us, playing right in the middle of the sold-out room. When the song kicked in, the rest of the band hit it from the stage, and it ended up being this wonderfully electric moment as we took in the energy from the room and the thousands of fans in attendance that day. It was an incredible event, and I'd be lying if I said that the feeling I get in my stomach when that banner drops at the beginning of our set isn't one of the most powerful adrenaline rushes in the world for me.

The very next night I played my first solo set to another sold out crowd, this one made up of not only my dear and loyal fans, but with my brothers/friends/family/bandmates watching from the wings of the stage. They had all had some drinks that night and were lovingly giving me a hard time - like my own private hecklers. But them being there was really a huge deal to me, and I felt very protected during an intensely vulnerable moment. It was an awesome bonding experience to have those guys at my side. At the end of the set, they carried me off the stage and into the crowd, who then hoisted me over their heads, carrying me from the stage to the bar at the back of the room. It was absolutely ridiculous (and a little embarrassing), but my heart was completely full that evening and I will never, ever forget how that felt.

For the remainder of that tour, it was just Oise and me on the road. I was booked for a string of small venue shows, playing sold-out crowds with nothing but myself and a guitar on stage. It was honestly a hands-shaking, full-on flushed face, terrifying feeling of being naked and vulnerable, and I had more nerves than I had ever felt in my entire life. I knew it was an important next step for me, but sitting backstage alone before and after each show without my brothers (or anyone at all) by my side forced me to confront my emotions and chew them about until I could digest them properly. Much like I imagine going to therapy must be, it was an incredibly necessary, but intensely horrible, process. When I was a kid in Pensacola, there was a long, circular driveway in the commune, and it was paved with nothing but broken oyster shells. At the beginning of the summer, we would run across it in our bare feet, trotting from one house to the next, and the pain was palpable. By fall, we likely could have walked on hot coals without flinching. This was a lot like that, I guess. I had to experience the pain of it until I became callused to it. Oise, as usual, knew what he was doing, though...if I had brought in musicians to play alongside me in that first run, I would've missed those critical steps in my journey because I wouldn't have been forced to sit with some very important feelings.

    I really wanted to bring more of my backstory to the live shows and decided that I would spend a little time speaking to the experiences that gave birth to the songs during my set each evening. I knew I would go into each show saying something, but hadn't really decided how deep I would go with it. I ended up bleeding out far more than I expected, and anyone who attended that first tour will likely confirm that I had a tough time getting through "Echoes" every single night. It was always at the same place – in the second verse where I come to the line *"Here in my heart, I've carved the words 'You don't own me.'"* I struggled with that line each and every time, my voice breaking as I (often unsuccessfully) fought back my tears. At that point in my journey, I wasn't sure I really even believed the words coming out of my mouth, and I was sincerely working through trying to speak them into existence every night.

I came home from that week and crashed out <u>hard</u> mentally, even more so than I usually do after a tour. I don't know that I can accurately explain the intensity of those first several days after returning home - it happens almost every single time, and it is wildly bleak. The plane rides back to the United States are honestly nerve wracking as I brace myself for the impact of slamming into my emotional wall a day or two after landing. Sometimes I am able to save myself from these crashes before they bottom out, and sometimes I can't. But it typically begins with a raging headache and overwhelming exhaustion, shortly after which, my mental state is obliterated into a terrifying place. I can only assume that the crash comes from returning to a bit of chaos after the well-oiled, well-ordered machine that is Tour - you know when to wake, when to eat, when to practice and where to be for every hour of your day. Then, you get on stage and work out your emotions night after night after night. The stage becomes your therapist's couch, and you get to artfully speak your pain, anger, love, hate and fears to the world, leaving you blissfully lighter than when you stepped onto it. When that is over, though, there *is* no schedule for me to keep, no avenue for exorcism, and I feel a sincere loss of purpose. People like to refer to depression as simple sadness, but for me it is a complete, all-consuming numbness; nothing matters, nothing has meaning, and I just want to sleep non-stop. I feel like I am spinning out of control, and I am embarrassed to admit that I often lash out at the people who love me and need me most. Like a wounded wolf, I become short with them, snapping and snarling - wanting to be alone but not wanting to be left alone because alone is much, much worse. I always feel incredibly guilty and angry at myself for doing it to them, but in the moment, how do I explain that it hurts to be needed while I am in a tooth-and-nail fight for my life?

During these episodes, I become especially

susceptible to toxicity, like an open wound would be prime for infection. I find that it becomes very easy for me to be drawn into destructive spaces, and the more there is going on, the more exposed I feel. The need for quiet regeneration is critical, and once I have that bit of space to reset, I begin to snap out of that negative spiral. On the other side of those valleys, I always work hard to show my love and appreciation for those that put up with me time and again during the storms. I know I'm a lot, and I am lucky to be loved in spite of it. The crash after this particular tour was a hard and desperate fall, but I am happy to say that after bouncing back from it, I rose higher than ever before. I don't apologize for how cliché it may sound, but rock bottom truly does leave us no place to go but up.

There Is A Light

On April 2nd of 2018, I went through a self-imposed "Unmasking." I shaved my beard clean off, lifted my head high, and went to war with my body, my emotions, and all that sought to destroy me. I made a decision to no longer put my brokenness on a pedestal. No more wearing masks to cover my debilitating depression. I said "no more" to spinning out of control and made a genuine and firm decision to take responsibility for where I was at and where I was headed. I had hit an emotional rock bottom and I felt utterly beaten to a pulp. I was exhausted, lost and becoming numb to the joys in my life. Often when this happens to people, it goes one of three ways:

1) Person says "fuck this" and gives up, ending their life immediately.
2) Person says "fuck this" and gives up, ending their life slowly.
3) Person says "fuck this" and makes an effort to change.

I was falling into category two, allowing negativity to run me over and take my control from me. I had completely given up and was scaring both my family and myself. I hated how I felt and knew that if I didn't make an immediate change to my attitude, I was going to be somewhere dangerous and alone. One day, while lying in that proverbial pool of blood, I woke up and felt a spark. It was a charge I am not sure I had ever felt before, and I found my passion again remembering my own words –

"To find Strength when your legs are too weak to stand.
To Persevere when all hope is lost.
This is what defines us. Not the roller coaster of joy and struggle, but the times we are mauled by life. The times

that would leave mere mortals begging for the cold quiet
solace of the grave.
Those that say no.
Those that refuse to be taken so easily-
Become gods of themselves.
I HAVE SEEN THE FACE OF DEATH AND WITH A
DEFIANT LAUGH SPIT IN HIS EYE.
YOU CAN'T HAVE ME, I'M NOT FUCKING DONE
YET!"

    I didn't want to go out miserable, defeated and a slave to all that sought to break me. I couldn't do that to my wife and my children. My parents. MYSELF. Once that beard came off and I took an honest look at myself in the mirror, I was horrified. I was bloated and wearing the body of a man with one foot in the grave. My eyes were hollow and dark. Haunted, even. Staring at the shell that was me, one that I didn't recognize at all, was a sobering experience. I immediately made changes to what I ate and started moving my body. This became an impetus for an incredible change that has benefited absolutely every area of my existence.

    It took me all of 46 years to admit to myself that, although I have made some poor choices in who I surrounded myself with in life, there is a very real probability that a part of me has been just as toxic, albeit differently so. As you may have gathered this far into the book, my toxic self came in the form of being a bit addicted to the comfortability of abuse and conflict and to the chaos of life. It came in the comfortability of wearing my sadness as a trophy (as many artists do). The comfort came in the form of strife, anxiety, anger, and sorrow...none of which felt GOOD, but they felt safe to me. Since I didn't believe that I deserved love, happiness or celebration, I often subconsciously attempted to sabotage those things in my life. Maybe a bit of that kill-or-be-killed ideal, who knows. One friend even jokes with me that I was an "emotional adrenaline junkie," which sounds comical until I dug deep and realized it's pretty spot on.

During the course of writing this book, I asked a few people who know me better than anyone to answer a question for me: *"What do I need to know about myself that I don't already know, either positive or negative?"* All but one of them mentioned that I am visibly drawn to conflict and chaos and that it seems as if I am unable to help myself from chasing after it. One of them even related it to smoking cigarettes, knowing full well it would kill you but still lighting up anyway. I cannot tell you what an important a part of my growth process it was to ask that of them and be open to their responses. It sincerely helped me understand myself and validate that a suspicion of mine about myself was a reality and, therefore, could be rectified. I wasn't (completely) crazy, which allowed me to empower myself to make changes to be better and, in turn, led me to *feeling* better. I would absolutely encourage everyone to try this exercise with their loved ones. Be open to hearing both the hard truths and any words of encouragement (offering to return the favor), and you will find yourself with an understanding like never before. Armed with these answers, I felt so much more prepared to face down my demons and fight for my light.

Our hearts are like petri dishes – if we give space to negative energy and hold it close, it will fester and grow in that warm shell until it becomes a disease feeding upon itself, overtaking everything around it. So, I made a conscious effort to be mindful of not only what I put in my body that was toxic, but also to pay more attention to what I was feeding my mind and heart that was toxic. I worked hard to say "no" to connections with those who did not lift my mental state. I worked hard to clear out anything that took but did not give. I worked hard to pay attention to my energy state and how that was affected by people, places or situations as well how it impacted not only myself, but those closest to me. As much as I wanted to, and as much as I will still likely die trying, I understand that I cannot and should not fix or help everyone I meet who may need or want something I can offer. Even admitting that in print here and now is a struggle for me because it feels like failure. I'm trying to learn to see this much in the way flight attendants instruct their passengers on how to handle a loss in cabin pressure – place the mask over your nose and mouth first and continue to breathe normally before helping others secure their own. I cannot "fix" myself by fixing others. It also serves me no purpose to continue trying to distract myself from my own pain in the work of "fixing" others, especially when that work breeds chaos and negativity. But, it *is* OK to just want to help for the sake of helping because I want to see others succeed. What's important for me to keep in the forefront of my mind and stay accountable to (all of us, really) is that we need to stop trying to put a mask over the nose and mouth of those looking to deplete us of our life supply in order to save only themselves. It's difficult. Trust me, I know.

Getting rid of my personal Facebook page shortly after the Unmasking was a freeing move for me personally that I do not regret. For one, it meant some distance from the noise which did not provide positive energy. It meant less temptation to be pulled into arguments waiting to be had. I realized that the platform and the distraction it brought had become a nuisance that was taking more than it was giving. I made the decision to kick my personal pages to the curb and bring more of my personal self to my art pages. No more dividing lines. This allowed me to, in turn, make my music more personal because it didn't come from a separate persona. It is honest and real. I don't need people to follow me as a person; I need them to see that my art and I are one in the same. It has always been important to me to be approachable and that my fans feel as though they can reach out to say "hello"; I didn't want to lose that. I also made an effort to bring more real life to my posts – even when real life was kicking me down. That meant sharing my hard days and downswings just as honestly as I would celebrate the good things. I wanted people to see that I, like them, am a real person with real struggles. I didn't want my secrets to keep me sick anymore, and I had way too much to do to stay sick.

In May of that year, just a few weeks after I began making my life turn around, I headed back to Europe for my second run as a solo artist. This one was wildly different, and we had been planning it since the moment I returned from the first one just months before. Unlike that tour, this one would invoke a completely different presence with locations that were perhaps less intimate and "homey," but were magical and unique and would completely immerse anyone in attendance in moods rich not only in sound, but in sight. To make it even more special, we brought along other musicians to join me on stage. I wanted to ensure that anyone who had come to an event on the first tour would be treated to something completely new, and graduating the songs themselves was important for that journey. To handle keys and additional guitars, I invited Ben Christo, a talented musician I had admired for many years, to join me along with Isabelle Klemt, whose cello work brought extraordinary life to the live show. I am still in awe of some of the locations we performed that month. Knowing how remarkable the events would be, my team and I decided to record a live album from the shows in Wiesbaden, which took place in a breathtaking historical church, and in Iserlohn, an evening spent playing underground in a natural cave to an intimate crowd.

When I flew in a day before the first show, Ben, Isabelle and I met at a small practice space to get to know each other and begin working out the logistics of the set. Much like my first time in the studio with Pete, I realized immediately that I had never really run a practice like this before, and I sort of shrank back into myself and let them take charge. Strangely, despite the fact that it was my tour and my name on the marquee, I almost didn't feel like it was my place to take the lead. What I did know for certain that day was that the two of them were going to be the perfect support system for this section of my journey, both musically and emotionally. They both provided me a great comfort on the stage, and I felt protected inside some very vulnerable, very public moments. It brought an invaluable peace that helped me lift my head a little higher than the tour before as I learned to stand on my own. And it was honestly really nice to not have to sit alone in my emotions after the shows this time. I think we gave people some beautiful evenings in that run, and I will hold a special place for what those shows with those people allowed me to do to move myself forward.

As it turned out, the live album from that tour was extremely popular, and my first pressing sold out in just four days. It was important to me to capture the stories I told in between songs so that if anyone who could not be at one of those events wanted to know more of my heart, they could have the opportunity to learn it in the album. For me, having those speeches (invocations as I called them) documented in such a way allowed me to reach more people who had experienced similar trauma and let them know they are not alone. It allowed me to document a pivotal part of my journey during which I stood up and spoke my traumas to the world so that I could begin the work of removing their power over me. It was a move to mark the end of an era.

Protein Powder Is The New Black

As I'm sure many others do after achieving a distinct physical transformation, I have been asked over and over again how I achieved my results. I thought it would be helpful to document the tangible changes I have made for anyone who may be intrigued or who might be looking for ideas as a starting point for their own plan. While there is no right or wrong way to do this for yourself, there are certainly HARMFUL ways, and it is important to note that what worked for me may not work for you. It is my way, and I worked through several different personalized plans before finding my rhythm within my body. All that said, feel free to skip this chapter if you don't want to hear that you really *should* quit pizza and beer.

I fully admit that, until recently, the self-help craze and the obnoxious health movement used to seem utterly stupid to me. In fact, there was a time where I was so far within my darkness, I couldn't even stand to see strangers smiling when I was walking down the street. I would see them and think: "The fuck are you smiling for, you maniac? Just walking around smiling for no god damned reason?! What is wrong with you?" I was so miserable with myself that I couldn't understand how people could be so effortlessly happy or well-adjusted, even though I desperately wanted to be that free. Some of you may have heard me offer the expression that "happy people let others be happy," a pillar I have been working hard to invoke. Somewhere at the start of this fight for my light, I realized that there is a very cyclical and symbiotic piece to genuine happiness. It is fed by good things around you and within you, traveling the expanses of your heart and mind until it just radiates back out into the world, where those who need it most can feed upon it, too. I wanted to be healthy enough mentally and physically to be someone who could light up myself and others AND be lit up by those who inspired me.

Many people get stuck on the idea that it is a lack of motivation that stands between them and their goals, but I think quite often it is more so a lack of discipline that prevents them from being successful (in whatever way they may define success). Motivation is easy - it comes to us as an idea. A want. A reason. Discipline is just the repetitive act of showing up every day (or as often as you feasibly can) and pushing towards your goal, even when you don't want to. Motivation is the heart; discipline is the action. Taking ownership of the garbage-in/garbage-out philosophy was the very first gift I gave my mental and physical health. And to stay accountable, I partnered with those closest to me and we took on the challenge together, as a pack. I said goodbye to sugars, pizzas, beers, heavy foods, processed foods and everything else that was doing anything but fueling me. I began eating six small meals a day, choosing foods that were clean, and focused on sensible carbs and high proteins. (Vegan friends: No need to add animal proteins, there are some incredible vegan protein supplements out there you can try that will still align with your ethical interests!)

While my physical transformation was QUICK, it was not easy. A lot of the changes came immediately with just the difference in my food intake alone, and it was amazing to see how much of my symptoms eased in a matter of a few weeks. There was even a period where I felt a little ill and off-kilter as my body worked to detox the garbage I had been feeding it – a sure sign that I was doing the right thing for myself. I also made a firm decision to make movement a priority, which gave me both physical strength and incredible mental benefits. Exercise became my job. Much like writing or playing, it became an absolute non-negotiable for my emotional health. Does that mean I don't indulge in a less-than-perfect meal or occasionally go a handful of days without working out? No. It simply means that I made a contract with myself to move my body and eat better. That's it. I don't know the science of it all, but dammit the magic of endorphins is real, and it has given me such incredible surges in my mood and creativity. There's a spark that occurs for me on the treadmill or lifting weights or being outdoors, and I have never once left the gym feeling worse than when I walked in. (My wife will no doubt attest to the shift in my mood from pre to post workout. It's pretty impressive!) Once that rush kicks in, my brain clears of the fog and my ability to focus, create and find a happy center is electric. Even (and sometimes especially) on tour, I have found incredible value in forcing myself to hit a hotel gym or do simple exercises in my room at the start of the day.

While simply working out will not cure clinical depression, I can assure you that your mental health won't suffer *more* with a little exercise. I know all too well that some things can't simply be walked or exercised off, and, if that is something you struggle with, I ask to you please share that with a loved one and plan a method of attack with your doctor. No treadmill in the world will fix chemical misfiring in the brain or body, but it CAN help light you up, putting you in a good place to be even more receptive to whatever route of therapeutic medicines or practices you find helpful. As far as movement goes, my only ask is that none of you go at it forcing yourself to do a type of workout you think you need, but wholeheartedly hate. There's really no point in setting yourself up for misery, failure and disappointment. Try many styles and go with what makes you feel accomplished at the end of it. And for the love of Christ, don't do that weird thing where you work out so intensely that you vomit and then wear that as a badge of honor. Just, no.

Unpopular opinion: It's time to throw out the scale. It is the absolute worst judge of your progress and is extremely dangerous to your mental state. The way you feel in your body is the best judge of whether you're getting stronger, and when you are on the right physical path, you will know. I understand this is not easy for everyone because, for most of us, scales have been a tool used since birth to rate us in progress. However, there is a slippery slope there when you slide into a place where you no longer have control over how you are using it or how it affects your mood and drive. Someone close to me struggled quite a bit with eating disorders over the years, and I remember them telling me that they would step on the bathroom scale easily a dozen times a day. If one day water weight showed a number even a half pound above the day before, there was a cycle of self-punishment that occurred, resulting in some very dangerous behaviors regarding food and exercise. People get frustrated when they begin working out regularly and the number on the scale doesn't reflect what they believe it should be – forgetting that adding muscle affects weight, and that muscle is GOOD. That scale is getting in the way of progress and provides no real look at your success. Throw the fucking thing away. This applies to men and women alike, regardless of their relationship with food. What we are shooting for is the feeling where your mind hits a new zone, and you feel better and start to see yourself differently. I am a big fan of visualizing my outward facing success in progress photos and recommend others to do the same. No scale in the world will do that for you, so, unless you are a boxer, never step foot on a scale again. From here on out, you don't weigh yourself anymore.

  Here's where I make a few (more) enemies: You need to cut out the beer. You just do. And you need to stop drinking like you're still in college. I'm not saying you can't have the occasional glass of wine or mixed drink with a meal, I'm saying put down the liquid bread and know when you've had enough. Don't drink to the point of losing your inhibition. When that fuzzy feeling hits you, and your thirst-demons start yelling, "fuck yeah, party time!" it's time to stop. To be honest, it's probably time to stop about a drink and a half before that. If this seems preachy, I don't apologize. If this rubs you the wrong way, maybe take a pause and dig into why it bothers you so much. Why are you afraid to let it go? Humans tend to self-medicate in a lot of ways. Some very obvious; some subtle. One of the best ways to work towards mental AND physical health is to stop self-medicating. I am absolutely not saying that you should throw away your prescriptions with wild abandon, as only you and your doctor know what's best for you. I'm saying stop drinking, doing drugs, fucking strangers every night, binge eating, smoking, compulsively shopping or WHATEVER you may be doing in an attempt to manage or numb your emotional state. None of it is helping, and it's not *really* helping you forget. All it's doing is distracting you for a short time, and at 3:00 a.m. when you're buzzed and making a phone call you know damn well you shouldn't be, I will gleefully say I told you so. And I only know because I've been there, too. Getting clean and sober will suck, but discipline will make it easier over time. I promise you that you'll never face down your demons if you are numbing yourself to their presence. And, as has been my experience with my son, some dear friends, and even myself, no one is going to change for the better until they are ready. It's the duty of the rest of us to continue to love them how they are until their day arrives.

Guess what? As with anything else in life, there are most likely going to be times where you fall off and skip a day, or skip a week, eat an entire bag of potato chips, or even drink until you black out. That's OK. Stop punishing yourself. You are human. Forgive yourself and start over tomorrow.

The Prodigal Son Returns

In November of the year of the Unmasking, I did a short East Coast tour with Jack O'Shea of Bayside. One of the events we were invited to perform was a beautiful and intimate backyard show at a home in Gulf Breeze, FL - just 20 minutes away from the church commune I lived on during the time of my sexual abuse. Almost as soon as the show was announced, I started thinking about its proximity to my Stigmata and wondering if I should make a stop to see it with my adult eyes. While traveling, I kicked the idea to Jack and our booking agent Jamie, who, knowing my story, were both immediately supportive of the idea. After the show in Gulf Breeze, we loaded up and drove out to the site, grabbing the address from that one golden-haired friend who had protected me during those years of horror. I felt somewhat apprehensive about being on those grounds, but not enough to not take this once-in-a-lifetime chance to face down my past.

When we arrived, pushing past the "No Trespassing" signs, I was somewhat satisfied to see that it was not only abandoned, but in badly broken-down shape. The large field we used to walk through to get from the trailer park to the church was very overgrown, almost forest-like now. The dorms that housed the bible college students, the dorms where my abusers laid their heads at night, were crumbling and worn with years of secrets and sin eating the buildings from the inside out. It was a ghost town, and I think if I hadn't been so far into my healing at that point, I would have been freaked out by the silence. But as it were, there was nothing these skeletons could do to scare me anymore. When we left that evening, we walked back to the van in silence. While I felt gratified, it felt somehow unfinished.

The next morning, we woke up early and I decided

to head back for one last look. The space was even sadder in the morning sunlight, showing just how horribly the years had laid in upon the structures. I grabbed my guitar when we parked, having a sudden and urgent need to play "Echoes" somewhere within these 27 acres. After staring again at the dormitory windows, I walked a little further until I saw the prayer room and knew - this is where it had to happen. Right here, outside that horribly stifling room carpeted in shame and guilt, dark and stale with sweat and dust. I stood outside the tiny building, hyper-aware of my surroundings at first, and started to play. The further into the song I got, the more I sank into it, singing the words right into the cracks in the paint; right into the gaps in the doorframe; up and over the tiny steeple. And when I was finished, I stood only a moment before turning on my heel and walking away.

<u>One thousand and ninety-five days reclaimed.</u>

I'm A Working Title, That's For Sure

I am not a great singer. Technically speaking, I am no better than someone walking down the street who only sings in his car or shower. BUT...I have a voice that is my own, and you know it is mine when you hear it. My musical gift is that my voice, my words and my presence on the stage invoke emotion in people. In this case, it is an honor to say that I am not a great singer. To me, perfection is boring. It is beige. When I meet my life's end, I hope that I slip away knowing that people were moved by what I gave of myself; that I stuck in their heart, not just in their head. I hope I'll know that I helped others learn something about themselves, and that together we embraced our imperfections as trophies we hoisted above our heads in pride.

Despite all my idiosyncrasies, I am the most "normal" when I am working on music. The process of creation carries a very calming routine for me, and outside of my family, it is the one thing that has been a constant source of stability and strength throughout my life. When a song idea comes from my soul, it is urgent and I have to release the notes from my fingers and lungs *immediately* in a near-frantic emotional purging. There's a laser-focus I have with my music, which is the complete opposite from my typically ADHD-driven method of bouncing around and leaving things chronically unfinished. I can put the idea down crudely on my phone (capturing its purest and most-raw feeling), put it away to breathe and later come back to it to craft the notes into what they tell me they are meant to be. I work them diligently until they tell me that they have finished their transformation. I've been told I make it look easy. It's not. It's painful and maddening, like a continuous cycle of heartbreak and falling in love, but it's a necessity and I don't have the ability to not answer that calling. I simply know no other way.

When I look back at my musical journey as a solo artist, I can trace the line of everything I have done in steps; a steady progression towards growing into my own. I never wanted to be just another dude with an acoustic guitar because that's simply not who I am as a person. I wanted whatever I did to be emotionally driven, honest and centered on finding myself, both as an artist and as a human, which for me are one in the same. The Casting Out, Nathan Gray Collective and even I AM HERESY were each a turn on my roadmap, intertwining and documenting my very real, oftentimes very messy, walk through this crazy life. From raucous party, to aggressive ceremony, to testing the brackish waters; each project encompassed necessary forks in the road on the way to where I am now, which is a vulnerable reflection of my purpose in this world and the work I've done to be here.

Just after the "Unmasking" (a handful of months after *Feral Hymns* was released), I began writing my second solo album. The transformation of songs from start to finish on *Working Title* ended up being monumental in comparison to what those on *Feral Hymns* and the EP went through, due largely to the fact that in between those albums I taught myself not only how to trust my own talents, but how to record on my own as I wrote. These two gifts became the biggest I have ever given myself as an artist, and it empowered my sound to finally and firmly show itself. As someone who is admittedly horrible with all forms of technology, handling my own recording during the writing phase is something that I am extremely proud of. Taking control of it allowed me the opportunity to try and fail until I learned to succeed at my own hand, and it has been more rewarding that I could have ever dreamt. It empowered me to take risks, try new instruments and push my own boundaries. I gave myself room to do it, and I fucking did it. I could lay down the bass, the vocals, the guitars and the piano with ease. I could even digitally add in the drums and cello, giving a well-crafted foundation for what I wanted to achieve in the studio. It was like an entire new world was born within me, and I was just completely at home in the work of it.

My sound really began finding itself once I could tap into my imagination and bring the music that lived within my lungs out into reality. I am magnetically drawn to the hook and melody of songs, and I love that I have come full-circle as a solo artist, reclaiming a sound that is true to myself but got lost in my heart's aching. When I stopped pushing myself to fit into places that were perhaps not entirely intuitive to me, my natural sound showed itself to be a brighter power-pop style that drives from all sides like a symphony, layered with nods to Midwest old-school bands and peppered with a touch of a Sunday worship vibe. This has always been the style that naturally comes out of me, but not always what I had the capacity to bring to fruition. I had really attempted to create that with The Casting Out, but I missed the mark when I started getting caught up in my emotional distress and allowed too many cooks in the kitchen. The sound got overly polished in the end, and, in an attempt at course-correction, I tried to back us off it on The Casting Out's self-titled album, but then the sound just got too loose. (Price I paid for not trusting my own instincts, I suppose.)

Artists like Rick Springfield, Hüsker Dü, the Replacements, the Buzzcocks, R.E.M, the Gin Blossoms, Green Day, Samiam, The Clash (whose first album was where I realized that punk wasn't just some pre-marketed rebellion) and even The Ramones, who, in my opinion, had catchy hooks but not much to say, all played a part in me finding what styles caught my interest. I realized that punk could be simplistic and rebellious while still having a hook, which was what I was most drawn to creating. And as far as lyrical content goes, the most rebellious thing people can do these days is talk about love and caring and kindness in a world pushing hate and fear and ignorance. I need what I do to matter to someone out there besides myself. I need to inspire others to take up the biggest rebellion of all – loving themselves, no matter what. That seemingly small act is the catalyst by which we can influence nations to be better. To care more.

The split EP that I released in August of 2019 with Jesse Barnett of Stick To Your Guns was the perfect bridge between *Feral Hymns* and *Working Title*. It was just three songs long, but provided a story-telling journey into where I was when I wrote *Working Title*. My first album was largely about me testing the waters, finding my way and figuring out how to be the artist I knew I had in me. The EP provided a peek at the journey I was taking personally and professionally by gradually stepping up the sound into something more sophisticated and allowing the lyrics to speak more about power *gained* than power lost. Even that recording experience was worlds different than with *Feral Hymns* – it FELT like the beginning of me letting go. It was more straightforward, I knew what I was getting into as the leader this time around, and I felt empowered to stand up and run things more. Because I had learned so much about the recording process itself, I came in with a plan, fully armed and in control. Not only did I enjoy the process of creating the full spectrum of these albums in the writing of each and every layer; the reward was greater than ever before. When I sent what I had to Pete Steinkopf while we were planning the studio schedule to record *Working Title*, I was insanely proud to hear him say: "Hey man, this is done. Just a couple of small tweaks, but you've done everything that needs to be done already." It was a moment that will stay imprinted in my spirit as one of the proudest accomplishments in my life.

While the work of recording at home soothed me, pushing myself to uncomfortable places in the lyrics did not. It never does, really, but the work is necessary and I drug myself back, kicking and screaming, to revisit some unresolved feelings. I have never cared for KoRn as a band, but many years ago, Chad had me check out a song they did called "Daddy." In this song, Ross Robinson, the producer for the album, had pushed Jonathan Davis into his emotions so much that you can hear his voice breaking and him crying on the song. It was exactly where he needed to go to get the mood across for a piece dealing with some intense situations. Similarly, in writing my own songs for this album, and even this book, I really had to challenge myself to touch wounds old and new. And while a lot of the tracks on *Working Title* and the EP started out very sorrowful and heartbroken, as I got stronger, the songs did too. I was able to reclaim my power as I wrote, the process of creation being more therapeutic than any shrink's couch could ever be for me.

Often, I am sincerely shocked at the transformation of songs, the change coming quite organically as I work through and resolve a particular feeling that the song may touch. For instance, the bridge I wrote in "The Fall" from *Working Title* started out quite sorrowful and broken, but as I kneaded and crafted it in tandem with my own healing, it ended up providing a tongue-in-cheek ownership of a situation that at one point felt completely out of my control. Ironically, "Refrain" was the only track on that album that started faster-paced and upbeat and ended up being a very pulled-back version of itself. Now, I can't imagine it any other way than what it became. So too, myself, I suppose. None of this transformation came easily, though, and I admit to several times at my home-studio setup when I would push myself to the point of sobbing in order to pull out and capture an emotion, needing to conquer it in my heart, but retain a mood to tell the story.

For all the wonderful musical partners I have had at my side in my life, at 46 years old I finally realized that I didn't need to keep passing my ideas over to someone else to complete, enhance or make "better" as I wrote my music.

No more fear of passivity. No more "Deja Coup" treatment. No more working on someone else's timeline, and no more feeling at the mercy of ideas in conflict with my own. I will always be happy to invite talented artists to join me in the studio or for a live show, but when it comes down to the creation of my art, it is born from my own blood, sweat and tears. And I could not be happier.

In a time of year that my mental health normally tips downward with the shorter, colder days and limited ability to be outdoors, writing *Working Title* was an invaluable distraction. It allowed me to create something wonderful and positive and life-affirming instead of simply passing the time in strife somehow. Recording for myself gave me a task that was a healthy and productive focus. A puzzle to complete. It gave me a vessel to finally and truly get out the ideas I had in my head instead of describing them to someone else and hoping they got the feel of what I was after. I think back to that 12-year-old me, writing albums in his head and crafting paper sleeves, and wonder what kind of magic he would've made if he had believed in himself enough to pick up instruments and figure things out. I finally get to live and die by my own abilities. After all the hard work I put in on my mental and physical health, my rewards were shown in the output of songs for *Working Title*. They were shown in my sleep pattern, my physical strength, my relationships and my ability to pull myself out of bad days quicker than ever before. For the first time that I could sincerely ever recall, I had hope for peace within myself. And although I know it is something that I will continue to fight for as long as I live, I am finally healthy enough in body and mind to have a fair fight. This is the only battle I am interested in getting bloody for anymore.

Emperor, Meet King of Cups

On March 17th, 2019, I played my largest solo show to date. It was in a large church in Bochum, Germany, and by that night (the last show on the tour), I was so much more comfortable with the technical pieces of the show that I was free to be more present and in the moment. My fingers were moving more instinctively across the guitar strings, and I could let go a bit, knowing Ben and Isabelle would do their part to support me. That evening was so special to me. At the end of the show, I broke into tears, shaken that so many people had come out to invest some of their precious time on this Earth in me. It feels to me now like the evening was a dream, the edges of the memory soft and translucent, but in that moment I felt like I was right where I was meant to be in life. The symbiotic healing that occurred there was monumental, and it helped give me the confidence to keep taking risks and keep telling myself "yes" when my inner-voice said "no."

I think people are generally inspired by those willing to put everything on the line for their dreams and their beliefs - at least for me, those are the types of humans who inspire me most. Those who dare to chase their greatness, even while most likely doing so in fear and uncertainty, light a fire in people around them, giving a gift of hope. Somewhere during my journey in this life, I came to understand that that brand of inspiration is not only my *own* talent, but my purpose. However, I learned the hard way that there is an extremely delicate line that must be walked for creatives such as myself who heal, thrive and make a living off of baring their soul. There HAS to be a recharging, and, until very recently, I haven't been doing a good job of that.

I had an incredibly insightful tarot reading in May of 2019 by my friend Sarah Potter. Just before I took the stage to play in Brooklyn, NY, she said to me: "You get on stage and eviscerate yourself. You slice yourself, spill your guts on the stage and people come and take pieces of you. It is healing for them, but how do you replenish yourself?" To which I replied, "I guess I don't." Until that very moment, I had never even considered this to be something that needed my care and attention, but it was dead on. As artists, we go through a blowing out of our darkest guts for our fans and often can't pick them back up. We find ourselves covering our mess to protect those we love from the carnage, leaving ourselves alone to clean it up quietly when they aren't looking. It can often come with an intense and overwhelming brokenness. Our art is our therapy, but if we don't allow those around us to help in our everyday life, we will end up with nothing left to spill out - a broken shell. The art is not just a simple therapeutic move, it's a bloodletting. And how much giving is *too* much while following that purpose? Every artist knows at some point they will be tapped out, but they still can't stop slicing - even when they are slipping on their own carnage. There's a quote by Soren Kierkegaard that speaks to this perfectly:

> *"What is a poet? An unhappy man who hides deep anguish in his heart, but whose lips are so formed that when the sigh and cry pass through them, it sounds like lovely music.... And people flock around the poet and say: 'Sing again soon' - that is, 'May new sufferings torment your soul but your lips be fashioned as before, for the cry would only frighten us, but the music, that is blissful.'"*

At this point, I like to think that the cyclical process of creation and performance recharges me. I admit that I sincerely hate relaxing because it means I am not tending to my self-defined purpose. I do recognize that this is a character flaw that may need tended to as I grow stronger, but at this time, being alone with my thoughts is something I am still learning to do. It is uncomfortable to me. A bit terrifying, if I am being honest. I can sincerely only do short bursts of downtime or it starts to bum me out, but I am learning to find peace in slowing down enough to live my life instead of allowing it to live me -and I am filling my time with much more positive activities. Being busy these days does look different for me, though; no longer is it a blanket I wear as a coping mechanism. It took firm diligence to grow towards a place where I was comfortable in chaos that was positive and not seek out toxic noise just to keep my head occupied. I don't have to *create* a space of misery in order to kick on my creativity anymore. Honestly, my own emotional ups and downs were enough all along, but I had never really recognized that as a medium I was in control of and could make work for me. When the downs come, and Jesus Christ they do, I allow myself room to feel it now. Once the dam somewhat breaks, I almost always kick into what I can assume is a manic state, and, as I mentioned before, that is generally when the remodeling, reworking, writing, playing, and most productive artistic adventures happen for me. Sometimes, my "ups" and their creativity spikes come on so suddenly, it can nearly be frustrating. I can be in a place like the hardware store and be frantically overcome with an idea that has to be exorcised immediately, no way around it. While it can become overwhelming at times, I'd rather be mad at myself for giving myself too much to do than for not putting my sail into the wind when it hits.

One of the things that has been at the forefront of my mind when it comes to creation and inspiration is how I want to approach the experience of my live shows. Like my sound, I want to be consistent in growth while maintaining a very authentic approach. I used to have a list of places I either wanted to perform or be recognized for performing.

Many of these, I am pleased to say, I have been crossing off over the years, including a printed appearance in Thrasher Mag (my young, skater-obsessed self fully impressed) and even a write-up in Rolling Stone. I have had the opportunity to perform in some absolutely surreal venues all across the world – churches, weird little Italian squats, underground caves, outdoor pavilions, festivals with a sea of people watching that went beyond even my line of vision, a shed in the middle of a trailer park in the deep South, gyms, VFW halls, intimate coffee shops, ships on the water, living rooms and gutter clubs. My ultimate pipedream, though? Playing on an episode of *Saturday Night Live*. (Hey – speak your dreams into existence, right?)

When I envision my perfect translation of myself into my art and my live show as a solo artist, though, it feels very warm, comfortable and genuine. It is more about the feeling the event invokes these days than the place it is held within. Home is many things to me. It is where I lay still at night, listening to the calm buzz of my family resting peacefully around me. It is the feeling inside the moment a creative spark hits my heart. It is stepping off the plane after weeks on the road. And it is on the stage under the warm lights. I would love to continue to perform my solo pieces with a full band of many moving parts that can be called upon for different songs. Much like Tom Petty or Rick Springfield, I want to deliver a full experience to those spending their hard-earned money and their precious time with me. I often daydream about how it will look - some songs delivered with just me and a piano, some with a trio of backup singers, others full and encapsulating with a wall of sound. I just want it all to be very special and safe. The ritual for me is about creating a relaxed and familiar space now – not about provocative imagery such as sigils, banners and skulls. I don't *need* to "remember death" anymore. I am comfortable right here - at peace in the rhythm of life itself, and I want to create an experience with my shows that reflects exactly that. I want you to step up to that stage in front of me and feel comfortable in your surroundings. To know that you can be yourself without judgement and let go of the day-to-day heartache you put yourselves through during the week.

 I want you to just feel like you can come home.

THE ELEPHANT IN THE ROOM

As I worked through this book, knocking down proverbial walls left and right, it was haunting my heart that I was still dancing around one barrier in particular, inexplicably afraid of ripping it down. I've never wanted to be seen as a man who asks others to (or supports others in their quest to) live within their truths while keeping his own tucked away. I have worked incredibly hard to be open and vulnerable because I genuinely believe that it is the only way to inspire others *and* work towards personal peace. While the desire to be open and free is there, the fear has often been crippling and loud. Paralyzing, even. But I have committed myself to moving forward in my second act of life, learning to accept myself as is, no matter what it takes. Working through just the more "comfortable" parts of that will never do me any favors, so - let's just do this, shall we?

I am very aware that questions, rumors and speculations about my sexuality have been whispered about on message boards and in darkened bar hallways for decades now. I do not pretend that I have always been forthcoming or open, and perhaps my silence and denial did more to feed it than quiet it. If you had asked me why I never opened up about who I am even a few hours before I penned this chapter, I would most likely have laid out a half dozen, half-assed reasons for you, none of which really outweighed the benefit of just letting go and stepping into the light. The truth is, when I was very young (well before my affliction occurred), I discovered that while I very much felt attracted to females, I felt similarly drawn to males. And although to me it was never a thing that felt wrong, over the years I wrestled with what society, the church, the scene, the men and women I dated, and those looking to explain away my sexual abuse might say. I think a large part of my keeping silent for so long was that I never wanted anyone to assume that I was who I was because of what had happened to me as a child, perpetuating a stigma that pours salt into the wounds of myself and every other victim of such abuse. It was quite the opposite, really. What happened to me only confused me more as I struggled to understand who I was at such a young age.

As I grew older and into an age of not only exploration, but one in which I had the emotional and physical capacity to be in romantic relationships, I entered into them with men and women alike, finding that I had genuine feelings for either at any given time. Not only that, but my life has been equally shaped and impacted by the relationships I have had with both women AND men, each teaching me in unique ways to understand and love myself and others. I will always hold special places for those who helped me feel free and saw me beyond whatever front I wore. For many years, I have fought with myself over how best to label who I am – gay, straight or bisexual. I am coming to view it in much the same way that I could never really explain or label what genre of music I belonged to; only that I have ebbed and flowed, and that I am simply an ocean beneath the waves.

In this place of life, I owe it not only to myself to stand in public with this piece of me; I owe it to every single one of my friends, my family members, loves past and present, and to my fans. I owe it to everyone who has stepped up to come out and show the world who they are too, or even those who might be wondering if they should. All my shouting for love, equality and freedom means absolutely nothing if I am not speaking up for myself as well.

I don't need to "Remember Death" anymore (to know how to live)

I am here to tell you that it is OK to custom-order inspiration, motivation and spirituality "a la carte." Back in May of 2017, I decided to very simply no longer associate with an organization I subscribed to. I learned a lot about myself during the time in which I did and gained some incredibly invaluable friendships through it. I just came to realize that the philosophy as a whole was not what I had been searching for. Much like any of the other ways of trying to make sense of the world and my place in it, it fell short. I have spent many years deeply conflicted, jumping all over the place in philosophy, motivation, desire and craft because I am truly so many people in one. I've been desperately trying to find where they all meet to find myself. Logically, I know that it is possible to be both fire *and* water, introverted *and* extroverted, lover *and* fighter, but somehow my heart has struggled to reconcile that. I spent many years fighting to define myself as belonging to something in an effort to feel a part of a movement bigger than myself – needing a sense of community, but not wanting to be boxed in by it. Perhaps some could mistake this as ambivalence, but for me, it is anything but.

On the other side of my "becoming," it has been very freeing to allow myself the ability to pick and pull the pieces that resonate with me from each vessel of understanding I have tried on in my life. It has allowed me to make my own melting pot of spirituality and reason; a kaleidoscope of ideals through which I can not only view the world, but through which I can reflect my light back into it. The truth is, my "end all, be all" did not lie in other people's theories, groups and philosophies, or in borrowed words and ideals that did not fulfill me. My self-created philosophy was much more meaningful to me than tailoring myself to fit within someone else's prescribed ideal. I continue to gleefully evolve the intangible for myself - choosing no particular side and being comfortable standing on my own. It is my hope that more people come to realize that there is strength in the grey areas and that they, too, decide to open their hearts to exploring many different ways of thought on their path to personal understanding. That they be open to building their puzzle with experiences and symbolism across a vast range of "–isms" and "–ists." Human beings are complicated; we just are. But no matter what lens we use to view the world, we are still human and still one of many. Let's leave less "us and them" in our wake. When we can approach life *itself* as a spiritual experience, we open ourselves to purpose and connection.

I think people like me who have seen behind the curtain are able to realize that there is no birth-written purpose for any of us; our purpose is to create it for ourselves (and sometimes others) as we go. And honestly, I think humans as a whole have been making it impossible for ourselves to get to our purpose. People don't feel like they matter in the grand scheme of things anymore, and often they become hateful, bigoted and willfully ignorant. This feeling is only exacerbated when we have world "leaders" who capitalize on our fear and subsequent misery, feeding both hysteria and hate. Typically, fear is born from a lack of control; a naturally born emotion put in place to protect us. When it is manipulated against us however, it becomes unbridled anger, and we find ourselves stuck in a cycle of lashing out - lost, confused and enraged. I truly believe that if we set our hearts to live with positive purpose, fear starts to dissipate and become powerless over us. That, simply, is how we win.

Social media is largely a mess right now, having disintegrated into a cesspool of negativity, doing more harm than good. YouTube, Facebook, Instagram, Twitter: each platform connects us globally while giving us a false sense of community and feeding our fears and insecurities. These platforms are connecting us with people across the globe, but are DISconnecting us from what is in our own backyard. Our own homes. I admit that I am just as guilty as the next of spending far too much time engaged in mindless banter and bored conflict through social media instead of using my voice for a greater good. It was a hard lesson learned when I realized that I have a responsibility to use my platforms for collective growth and healing and that *that* purpose needed my time and attention far more than I needed to engage in faceless arguments with people committed to disagreeing with me. In life, both on and offline, not everyone you come across is going to be someone you should devote energy to, negative OR positive – our time on this Earth is simply too precious to give away freely. (There IS a fun positive to social media spaces, however. When people give their stories back to me after I share something difficult, it sincerely keeps me going, and I love when I see conversations sparked in the comment sections of my Facebook and Instagram. It brings me joy to watch others build friendships and create communities together.)

With all the readily available ways to disconnect from ourselves and those we love, many of us find comfort, energy and peace in the chaos of life through little rituals that keep us going – personalized ways to play mind games with ourselves which allow us to hit a re-start button at any time and place of our day. This is something that requires no subscription to any particular faith (or lack thereof) and is a very normal, healthy way to cope and thrive, giving us back our power, safety and control. Colors have become important to me, for instance. (I notice that I always wear black shirts to the gym and white shirts on stage these days.) Light, sound and scent are also big ones, and I like to set the tone of my home so that it invokes warmth and safety, which I do through small habits that help set my mind at the ready. One of the greatest powers of ritual is that the act is very personal – you can make your own and it works just the same as whatever thing people in church pews have done for centuries to achieve that same sense of calm. Prayer, numbers, the outdoors, letters, timestamps, plants, meditation, fire-work, sleep, music, dance, written word, candles, crystals, coffee, make up, exercise - however you choose to manage the nonsense of life itself is yours to make personal, which is, in essence, what spirituality is. As long as what you do doesn't directly harm yourself or others, I am happy to back you, so long as it keeps you on track and helps you achieve that necessary transformation. Deep down, we all crave something to belong to. This sense of belonging to something (even if just to yourself) and the subsequent sense of control are instrumental in giving you purpose and feeding that creation spark that drives us all. That belonging makes you healthier, mentally stronger, emotionally resilient and spiritually aligned to whatever it is you seek in this universe. Simply put, it makes you happy, and damnit, happy people let other people be happy. We need more of that in this world.

For me, belonging looks a whole lot different these days. My community is much smaller and more intentional than ever before, and I only allow those I trust implicitly to take space within it - my family and a handful of very dear friends. This has allowed me to focus on what matters most to me as time inevitably makes its way into the second half of my life. Over the years, there have been people who felt entitled to my energy and time, and that has been frustrating. I have since learned that I was perhaps largely at fault, afraid of setting the right boundaries for fear of hurting someone else, instead, foregoing what it was that I myself needed. I am generally happy to share energy, time and space when it is symbiotic, but a goal of mine moving forward is to continue to be approachable while being a little more protective of myself so that I don't continue to get overwhelmed. It destroys me to have to do so because I know a large part of who I've branded myself to be is someone who is extremely available to my fans, but I often find I give people too much of me, inadvertently giving them false expectations. Or worse, I find that I have opened myself up to people set on using my light just to illuminate themselves or set on snuffing it out completely. This, like so many things, is a process, and I am working on it.

In order to be whole, to experience life with a positive heart and fulfill our purpose in this world, we need to come to the understanding that not only do we deserve a community that feels safe and empowering, but that as life ebbs and flows, we do too. It is within our power to experiment and try new things. What feels right today may not in a year from now, and that is completely normal. Never let anyone shame you for growth, change or for how you seek to belong. Nothing in life is "one size fits all," so go out and create the space you need to thrive. If you find peace, advocate for those who have not. Seek to understand. Be bold. Be caring. Be respectful. Keep your circles close, and carry each other when need be. Unplug. Sit by the fire together. Share a meal. This world is in desperate need of healing. Above all, please know that no matter what lies your brain may tell you, you are never, ever alone.

Seven Devils

A friend once asked me what my mental state goes through when I step on that stage, sharing with me that watching me during a boysetsfire set, especially, was like watching seven devils take me over. To be very honest, on that stage is really the only time I completely let go of the leash that tethers all the pieces of myself in. All those voices, all of those selves, my fears, hate, love, anger, sorrow… every single corner of me comes flying out. I know it is generally assumed that stage personas are fake, much like the way one would think of a salesperson trying to get them to buy a car they can't afford, but I contend that they are the realest selves an artist has. For me, each of those devils is a special, private part of me, being either invoked or shed at will, and often at a speed that dizzies me. What I do up there is absolutely manic - it has to be or it loses its authenticity - but it is also sincere. Part of my progress as a human has been in getting comfortable with not compartmentalizing pieces of my whole so that I am not streamlining myself on stage. Up there, I just simply let go…as soon as the first note clicks on, I am inside the moment and everything else falls away. I symbolically black out; it's the only place I feel truly present. In that space, I can't be shaken. I am safe and free, and whatever the outside world dragged me through that day/week/month/year fades away. I am both lucky and eternally grateful to have a place like that where I can let go. I know not everyone has a space and platform to achieve that for themselves, and I think that's why so many tortured souls walk this Earth. Before you ask, yes, I still get nervous every single show. It's more anticipatory nerves than fear, a place that took me decades to get to, but I vow to quit performing the second that feeling stops. I don't want a life that's comfortable enough to not scare me.

There's a really bittersweet aspect to being in boysetsfire right now. I'm honored that these songs of revolution still speak to people, but just utterly heartbroken that they are still relevant. At times it feels as if everything I am screaming is empty and shouted upon deaf ears because the changes I am calling for simply aren't being made, and the challenge I have thrown out is being boldly unmet. We as a society are still complacent, and we as a society are collectively responsible. We aren't owning our part in the solution anymore - it seems that many have simply shut down and backed away; out of sight, out of mind. We've grown older; we've grown tired. We've become hopeless and disillusioned. It's as if we are afraid to speak out and be standing alone, or afraid that we may misstep social boundaries if we do it "incorrectly." The revolution seems to have gone cold in our veins, and I'm sick of having to sing this stuff because it's not just "songs," it's our *reality* – it always has been. For me, when I step onto that stage, wrapping my entire core around itself, balled up and screaming until my eyes go bloodshot from venting my frustration and begging and pleading for hope and action, it sincerely breaks my heart to feel that it's all for nothing. And I see you out there, I feel you. I KNOW I am not alone, but I do fear that my words have become less anthemic and more nostalgic. More about a time in our lives when we cared more, fought harder and were filled with hope. But I refuse to give up, and I know there is a generation behind me (and one behind that) that has more power to change the world than we could have ever dreamt of when I was young. My duty now is to tirelessly continue to cheerlead the community in the hopes that it inspires the one person who CAN make change. I feel like I am failing if my message doesn't inspire others, and I am afraid that such a time is near. Although I will never give up, I do wonder how I can do my part better. To make it matter more.

I have seen and heard many of you pleading for new anthems in this time of political and social unrest. I need to be able to give 100% to whatever I am doing, and right now I just can't give that to writing for boysetsfire because I am all-in on the work that needs to be done for myself, hoping to change the world by starting in my own heart. I do genuinely believe that the changes we make on a micro-level, in ourselves, in our homes and in our communities, have the power to overtake nations. Love and hope always fucking win. Whatever boysetsfire puts out next can't be done half-assed and has to be better than anything we've ever released before, so if it has to wait a bit until we all arrive at that place, then so be it. I will never pour half my soul into my art, and I'm learning not to put that pressure on myself to try to give my all to too many things at once. I deserve that, as does my family, as do you.

Freedom Is A Mercy

Perhaps not surprisingly, the therapeutic effect of working on this book has been both joyful and intense, and I really had to challenge myself to sit in some uncomfortable emotions in an effort to work through them. I would say that, for the most part, I was able to stay steady; easily pulling my moods into a better place when I could feel them cracking from the weight of anxiety and total recall. There was a short stretch of days, however, where I could not.

I couldn't really put my finger on one single thing that kicked it off, but for nearly three days in the middle of the summer of 2019, I had an intense burning in my stomach. I was wildly cranky, couldn't sleep well, and just felt generally off and not myself. I can't even pinpoint exactly what emotion or feeling was choking me, but I was most definitely in a dark place. My cousin asked me to meet up with him for a drink one night, and I joined him at a small bar just down the street from our neighborhood. We sat talking for an hour or so (me having only water because the last thing I wanted to do was exacerbate my mood any further) and then we said our goodbyes. As soon as I got into my car in that parking lot, there was an overwhelming rush of emotion that swept over me, taking the air right out of my lungs. It came on very suddenly and very intensely, and I sat there sobbing in my car for a good 10 minutes, overtaken by a great sadness. And when it was over, I felt absolutely incredible. I don't even know how to accurately describe how deeply, darkly consuming those few days felt, but getting rid of whatever dense cloud that was left me feeling rejuvenated. In recalling the experience to a friend, I remember saying: "That was so weird. It was like removing a splinter…" and I stopped dead in my tracks as what I said was echoed back to me, freezing me with a strange chill, like that cold brush across the back of your neck when you feel like you're being watched.

Not long before this night, I was talking about how much Aleks loves wearing shorts and generally is of the mind that the less clothes he has to wear, the better, and mid-sentence, I was sucked back to a dark and difficult memory about hiding my bruised and rug-burned knees under pants, even in the middle of the summer. Just a few days later, we noticed him favoring one of his feet while walking through the living room and discovered he had a splinter in his foot. Being 5 years old and having a splinter removed is a colossal deal. As Katie and I spent a solid hour working with him to remove it while he thrashed, screamed and panicked, the intensity of the situation got the better of me. Once we finally rescued the sliver of wood, I slunk off to the bedroom to try to collect myself, fighting off the triggers that pounded deep into my gut that whole hour, leaving me on the verge of collapse. Something as seemingly simple as getting my child dressed, or trying to hold him still while he screams and fights, can dredge up horrifying feelings. Perhaps what I was carrying in that cloud for those three days had been switched on by this very normal parenting event, and I didn't even know it until it was gone.

As I sat there in my car after that release, stupefied by the irony of my comparing that experience to removing a splinter of all things I could've likened it to, I couldn't help but think back to that video for "Echoes" when the visible puff of air came out of my mouth and wonder if perhaps I was working out some sort of physical manifestations of my buried traumas. Whatever the explanation, I knew that I had just freed myself from something that was no longer permitted to take up space.

Almost immediately after that strange exorcism, and just days before I hit the studio with Pete, I found myself not only completely rearranging the order of the tracks I had laid out for *Working Title*, but writing a completely new song. With my mind a bit clearer, I suddenly felt like there was a step missing in my story, and it was hugely important to me that there be a steady progression from *Feral Hymns*, through the split EP and into *Working Title*. With the rush of energy that came after that night, "In my Defense," the first song that would be on the album, was born. My working was complete.

A couple of weeks before I headed to Asbury Park to record, I decided to try to play my first solo set with a full backing band. It was absolutely wild to see it all come to fruition, and as nervous as I was about how it would come together, desperate to test the waters a bit, it was absolutely breathtaking when it happened. When Rakus (who plays guitar and bass for us in boysetsfire), Jake, a friend of mine named Jaelyn and I got together to start running the set for that show, I was honestly a little concerned; I think they were, too. Practicing in the tin can that is Rakus' garage, it was difficult to envision the final product. But at sound check the night of the show, I immediately thought, "oh shit, this is going to be amazing!" and I could see a bit of relief on their faces, too. By the time it was our turn to play, I felt wildly confident and I was beyond ready; it was all I could do not to jump on the stage to help the band before me unload quicker and rush them off so I could begin my newest push forward. Bringing the full backing band to life and playing "Brighter" ahead of the EP release let me see how people would receive the new sound I was about to bring to my solo act, and I was elated with how it all played out. When we were done, I felt energized, confident and 100% ready for this new direction I envisioned.

My experience recording the album *Working Title* was absolutely beyond my wildest dreams. I don't know how to even begin to accurately express how healing and self-affirming those weeks were for me. The night before I began recording my vocals (absolutely glowing after five straight days of bass, guitars and drums), the wonderful revelation came to me that not only was what was coming together finally defining my sound, it was an actual reclamation of all that I let get lost in my quest to create The Casting Out. In the time and place in which I tried to give birth to that piece of me over a decade ago, I was an utter mess. Now - somehow, miraculously - I had gotten a second chance. A chance to really do this thing right. Somewhat organically and by happenstance, I had gone backwards to find myself, retracing all the steps I missed amidst my drunken turmoil, to pull my heart from the wreckage and go forward whole. And not only had I *created* a second chance for myself, people wholeheartedly made room for me to do so. Friends, family and fans alike encouraged me to take risks, dream bigger and push myself harder than ever before. I didn't fucking settle for "good enough" this time around. The bigger and brighter the sound became, the more I was able to use those songs as a vessel to dance upon the grave of my past and everything in it that sought to destroy me. I felt clearer and freer than I have in my entire life, and everything was coming together as it was meant to be.

To complete the full-band sound for the album, I brought back in musical artists who were not only dear friends, but could read me intuitively and take my leadership in stride. Artists who were incredibly talented at their craft and showed up without an agenda, coming together as a family to support me and this journey I am on. Rakus, Jake, Becky, Elyse, Ben and Jaelyn – each of them gifting a piece of themselves to this reclamation. Pete himself was a wonderful partner to help bring my vision to reality exactly as it was meant to be; there was no whitewashing of the emotions in my vocals, and he could anticipate my needs before I even had to ask. It still blows my mind how vastly everything transformed inside those walls as we worked together to bring out those songs. "Working Title" and "What About You" became bigger than my wildest dreams, walls of sound that made me stand taller than ever before. "Mercy" was translated as sweet and sorrowful as I wanted, and "Refrain" tapped into a raw exhaustion in a way that still shakes me to my core.

By the end of my time in the studio, I was more joyfully tired than I can ever recall being - mentally, creatively, and physically. I even experienced a mild crash about three quarters of the way through, gratefully collapsing into my home for 24 hours to recharge and rest my voice. I felt anxious, worn down and entirely self-critical, working incredibly hard to stay above the crashing waves. I was giving my entire soul to this album, and in 11 long days in the unforgiving Asbury summer heat, holed up in the basement studio that is Little Eden, I finally gave birth to my dream. By the last day of recording, I had absolutely nothing to add and nothing left to give, and I knew in my soul that I had finally found myself within my art.

Yeah, there is a light where the darkness feels no shame

There is a love that never has to fade

The Lovers, The Dreamers & Me

During the course of writing this book, I was asked what I was most excited about people learning once they've read it. At first, I couldn't even come up with anything - I got swallowed up in a mini panic attack thinking about how much of myself I was putting out into the world. Again. Fully. In my first book, I said a lot without saying it, dressing my pain in prose and dancing around my words. When I decided to write another one, I knew that this time I had to be very intentional about it – I had to do this the right way, or I would never achieve what it was that I had set out to do. Being vulnerable is never a fantastic feeling, but I held onto hope that I could shine a light for people to find their way to the other side, so this part of the process is deeply necessary. All I can do is speak my truths and share what I have learned in hopes that it helps others. So much of these lessons come back to one very simple and real statement for me:

Everyone and everything I thought I needed to be, I already was.

Love is calm. It is the peace within your chaos. Self-love, joy, allowing ourselves to love and be loved in return… these are the things that make us human. These are the arms we should be taking up. We cannot hate the hate in the world away. We cannot self-abuse, lash out and shame peace into existence. We cannot wish upon a falling star for faith or be passive with our hope.

Every bit of the darkness I have faced down in my life is a small part of my past, and I am proud to say that I am still here; at times shaken, at times changed, but never broken. Much in the same cathartic way I find release from playing a show, this book was intended to help me release and work through all that aimed to stand in my way. My healing has been a series of steps for me, and when I doubt my progress, I reflect back on that quote I mentioned earlier by Barack Obama: "better is good." It allows me to appreciate my small victories - every single important and valuable step that I have made. I do not pretend that I have not been through a lot, or that I am not a lot myself. I am able to look back now and proudly say that with constant pushing forward, I am better now than I ever was before, which is all any of us can hope for ourselves. Hope requires action or it sits stagnant in the air, nothing more than a wish you made over a birthday cake. Forcing myself to live in an uncomfortable space while telling my story and standing publicly vulnerable in the work of progress has not been easy, but it has let the wounds air out and showed me that none of us are struggling alone. I went from being completely walled off, to reluctantly peeling off my armor, to wildly hypersensitive, to breathing for the first time since I was no more than 9 years old.

    I think many of us who survive some sort of trauma prevent ourselves from moving forward because we subconsciously refuse to do so without some form of closure. If you are one of them, may I offer this: Self-empowerment is the closure you seek. It is in pulling a purpose from your ashes. I know that your trauma removed your power, but you CAN take it back. I am living proof. We <u>have</u> to re-wire our idea of closure and understand that it is not a thing we can (or should) get from others. If you ask for an apology and get it, you will always wonder if it was genuine. If you ask someone who hurt you to heal you, you are keeping them in power. The only true closure comes from cutting the cord. We have to stop that obsessive behavior in which we seek something that cannot be given to us. Forgiveness, an act that can be ritualistic, is not necessary for your healing. I promise you, it isn't. If you are not moved to forgive someone who has traumatized you, don't. You can hold onto the pain and emotion of what happened in order to not let the cycle repeat itself without holding on to the person who inflicted it. It's not the pain that you must let go of, it's the power the pain has over you. It's the place in which you are crippled by the pain at hand.

What I truly want for anyone reading my story, or attending one of my shows, or listening to my album, or simply passing me on the street, is to find comfort in the cycle that life presents us. Success is not a goal, and defeat is certainly not final – just a challenge for us to find another way. Another lesson waiting to be taken on, to grow from. All the ups and downs can be exhausting, I can attest to that in painful reality, but I think the secret to enjoying the complete life experience is in acceptance that it is, indeed, an experience. More still, that the "good" *and* "bad" parts are necessary in order for us to understand why we are here on this Earth. You do have an option and a choice of how your life plays out in front of you. We cannot change our pasts, but we can take charge of what comes next, so long as we can be bold enough to put down our swords and allow good things to come to us.

I know that your pain has grown over you like a blanket. Like a shield you have used to keep others out. Letting go of that can be nerve wracking, but doing so and honoring *yourself* with new, positive habits is invaluable. I promise you that you will find your way if you just hold on to a small bit of hope in those tough times - **there's beauty in your becoming, and you were meant for so much more than you can imagine.**

I believe that our secrets are keeping us ill and that secrecy and silence feed shame. This feeling can be beautifully healed by hearing: "I'm here for you" or "I know, me too." I have to believe that there WILL come a point where we (I) won't have to vocalize our (my) trauma so often because every time we shout it into the wind, its power lessens. Perhaps you, like me, find yourself instinctively touching your wound to see if it's healed over yet, waiting impatiently for your body and mind to do the work to scar over. I know that a day will come when we each finally recognize that we are not our abuse or our traumatic past – that it was a horrible thing that happened to us, but it neither killed nor defined us. We were bigger and stronger than the horror of it, and we were able to take our ashes into our hands and press them into diamonds. That external closure we seek? Time will take the sting off of the desperate desire for it, even if/when we don't actually get it from those who tried to destroy us.

In our darker times, we got used to negativity. We lived in fear, numbing ourselves to joy because we were afraid it would be taken away from us. I say it's time to start expecting the good things life has to offer. Let's let our guards down a bit – open the window so light can find its way in. Vulnerability is the cornerstone of confidence and healing. When you open yourself up to others, you feel your audience and it becomes a shared conversation that allows for symbiotic catharsis. Maybe your venue isn't a stage like mine. Maybe your audience is a party of one single person besides yourself, but that doesn't change the importance of the work you are doing. No matter *how* many times we've been burned by it in the past, opening ourselves up is the only way to welcome the love, care and inspiration we inherently deserve. Laying down our weapons is the opposite of weakness – it takes great strength to stand exposed and trust in the universe - *especially* with the knowledge that we cannot control the outcome, only how we feel about the outcome. I promise you that all you seek in life is on the other side of your fear and that you absolutely CAN do brave things while being scared. Get comfortable in your uncertainty. It is the only way through this.

Not everyone in this world is meant to understand you, however. In fact, it will be (and should be) quite rare to find someone that does, and you will most assuredly go through some painful trial and error to discern who, how and when people take space in your life. We've all given too much to the wrong people, desperate to be seen behind our walls, and there is absolutely nothing wrong with that - there is so much we can learn about ourselves in those times of openness. (Even more in the times we are broken and left alone to grieve.) Still, I believe that each and every one of us is deserving of love and celebration, and I can't wait to see who we grow to be within the homes we create with those who speak to our souls.

Grief looks like many things and is born from many hardships – like the loss of a loved one, the loss of a time in your life or the loss of yourself. No one is immune to it. It has no timeline, no standard, and no rulebook for when and how it shows up. Sometimes I think of all the periods in my life that I have found myself angry and self-destructive, hiding my sadness and fear behind a front of aggressive emotion. Or the times I was the life of the party, no one knowing that I was just desperately numbing myself to the horrifying movie in my mind. Sometimes allowing ourselves to heal from our grief is just as frightening as feeling it because we subconsciously believe that healing means we don't care anymore. We fear that if we heal, we don't care about the person we are mourning, or that we don't care that we were tortured and that our life was in some way stripped from us. We may even tell ourselves that being able to heal might mean that what happened to us wasn't as bad as we believed. In reality, healing means we care very much. It means we love ourselves enough to give ourselves the life we deserve in spite of our past. Please also understand this:

NO ONE CAN TELL YOU WHEN YOU ARE DONE GRIEVING. NO ONE GETS TO PUT A TIMELINE ON YOUR PAIN.

I am learning for myself that it is OK for me to move on now. You, however, can let go whenever *you* are ready. Just know that your pain is not who you are. Your trauma does not make you; the way you rise from it does. We cannot save ourselves from the hardships life may deal us, but we can choose what we do with them. And please understand that there's a difference between fixing yourself and owning yourself. Your place in the world is unique and invaluable. You are not meant to be fixed because you are perfect as you are: every rough edge, every manic corner. You are only meant to OWN who you are - as fully and completely as possible - in order to grab onto your happiness and fulfillment.

You are perfectly imperfect.

An Intercessory Prayer

One of the people whom I asked my "what do I need to know about myself" question was my father, who wanted to deliver his observations in person. On my 47th birthday, we sat together over a beer and he spoke to me for nearly half an hour without taking a breath. It was obvious that he had put a lot of thought into his answer (having ruminated on it for at least two weeks), and when he began to speak, I could see a weight lift off of him. Like everyone else whom I asked, he noted my struggle with my anger first. He said that watching me throughout the last several years has been like witnessing me work through stages of grief – denial, anger, bargaining, and depression – only acceptance eluding me. He told me he wants peace for me. At the end of his homily, he left me with a few final words that I found most impactful – our purpose is in the micro, not the macro. He told me that finding what and who we are to *ourselves* and the peace that comes with that will organically create a ripple effect out into the world around us. It is a statement I have taken deeply to heart, and will forever be grateful to him for sharing. I actually ended up getting some insight into my father himself that night, which left me feeling more in tune with the best way to love and care for him. So, that time together became a wonderful gift for us both. I know his wish for my personal peace is through acceptance of what happened to me as a child, but to be honest, I don't know what acceptance looks like for me yet. I imagine that when I am there, I'll just know.

I want people to understand that when I am shouting messages calling for hope, love and empathy, it is still a rally cry to myself, too. I know that I have been speaking a lot to these things as of late, but I believe with everything in me that they truly are the catalysts most effective for change. We can combat the darkness within ourselves and the world around us by approaching it gently with these three attributes as tools because change IS always possible. Sure, it is messy and difficult and challenges our patience and conviction, but it is possible... and so very worth it. When we ask others to look within themselves honestly and offer them an approach different than what is comfortable to them, we must do so with love, hope and empathy. Above all, we must humble ourselves to do the same and ask only of others what we ourselves are prepared to do. And while it is important to use discernment as to who and what deserves our energy, it is also important to know when to (or not to) let go or give up. We need to understand that there will come a point when we have done all we can and must let go, trusting that people will find their way as we stand beside them to simply offer support and warmth for their journey. "What do I need to know about myself that I don't already know?" Such a simple question, but more powerful than anything else I have ever considered to help empower myself on this journey.

In this new place of my life, I am noticing that the post-show adrenaline high is different than it used to be. Not so long ago, I would have jumped off that stage, said my hellos, and immediately sunk into whatever I could find to attempt to recreate that feeling. I would fill my time with empty actions that did not lift me up; often doing more to numb me or drag me down. As the years passed, I have learned to take better care of myself on the road, both physically AND emotionally.

boysetsfire just completed our 25-year anniversary tour, which was mind-blowingly and wonderfully insane and fulfilling from start to finish. The fact that we could not only put on our own festival (again!), but sell it out to 4,000 people while hand-picking bands to open the night for us is utterly surreal. It took a lot of work, a lot of sacrifice and a lot of luck to get where we are, and I hope that I never become numb to that magic. As the tour wrapped up just a month and a half before the release of this book, my second full-length solo album, and my third European tour, I made a concerted effort to be mindful of my energy for those two weeks on the road with my brothers. There was one particular evening in Munich where I broke down pretty intensely in the middle of our set while performing "Prey," and it absolutely rocked me to my soul. That song is extremely powerful and personal to me, and on that evening, I unraveled as the words hit me in the gut and triggered my ghosts, taunting them into my vision. I'm looking to learn to congratulate myself more in this place of life because every step of my road is an accomplishment. So, although it was intensely difficult for me to work through and stay above the feelings that evening dredged up, I was able to stay present and recover healthily, giving myself space to feel my pain. Not so long ago, I would have no-doubt slid out and undone all my hard work, looking for relief in some toxic way, self-medicating for days. I was proud to have been able to implement more positive behaviors on the road amongst the raucous on that tour, including how to maintain my peace, steam my voice diligently both before and after shows, and get a reasonable amount of sleep.

Before that tarot reading with Sarah Potter, I was in the mindset of, "I'm just giving myself therapy by doing this" when it came to my public evisceration on stage. I thought that all I had to do was bleed out and I had fulfilled my reason for existence. I never understood that I had to care for myself in the process. I now know when I'm missing some steps in my recovery and/or preparation, and am careful to give myself back the energy I put out up there. As I grow and change and step into who I was meant to be, I feel a certain responsibility to give myself the best shot at fulfilling my purpose for as long as possible, in the hopes to make the most impact. It is not only my responsibility to create MY purpose within this vast, monochromatic void of life; it is my responsibility to help those around me realize their OWN purpose in life.

Bluntly stated, life itself is meaningless and we each must create our own meaning within it. We have the power and ability to create our own purpose; it is neither a set blueprint for our path that is defined for us before birth, nor is it something that can be taken from us by trauma, or poverty or circumstance. Our meaning is ours to choose and chase freely. Our reason for existing on this Earth is ours to work for and ours to fight for. Whatever you do with your limited time in existence, I hope you build a space with something that sets your soul on fire. The purpose that I have created for myself is to pursue what I love with full fervor - which is music. It is to use my stage, both literal and figurative, to help others find their passion and light. To paint the dull canvas of life in my blood, sweat and tears in hopes that it will, in some small way, connect others, inspire others and heal others. Starting over at 47, I am continuously overwhelmed by the chance I've been given in this phase of life. I vow to never take for granted the opportunities I've had to grasp all that the universe has to offer and the space I've been given to be me. Unapologetically, genuinely me. I've worked hard to be where I am - musically, mentally and physically, and I could not be more proud to stand tall and have it welcomed by the world around me with open arms. Thank you for being here. Let's keep our eyes on the horizon and our heads held high. All that we dream is a reality if we just put our minds to it.

The Foreword

The shitty part about life is that we can't save ourselves or the people we love from having to experience pain and tragedy along the way. Each of us has a story. The most we can do is purge the pain in the hopes that we can become part of a community to grow in. To become one of many who not only made it out alive, but managed to thrive and create in spite of it.

My experiences and my place within the public eye have allowed me to start a conversation, and I have assumed a duty and responsibility to speak up because I have a voice and an audience. That said, if I can do this, anyone can. I know it's hard to be brave, but I promise if you speak, people will listen. No one, and I mean NO ONE can take your voice from you. They may threaten you, push you, taunt you, belittle you, humiliate you and try to tear you down, but they can *never* keep you silent. When you feel powerless, please, please remember that. I know that there are days when the words are at the tip of your tongue or fingertips and you go numb with anxiety and doubt, but I can assure you that your healing is on the other side of that feeling. And when you are ready to speak, we will listen. And we will believe you.

I recognize that the closest some people get to speaking their hearts' truths out loud is when they are singing and screaming along with me at a show. I want you to know that I see you and can absolutely feel your energy. I take it on in full as we push for that mutual catharsis, and I am honored to help give you your voice, even under the guise of my own:

<u>I see you. You matter.</u>
<u>Lift your head up and keep fucking going.</u>

Healing is not a destination for any of us to achieve; it's a (oftentimes exhausting) journey. I know how motivational-poster-cheesy it sounds to read that, but it's true. And although I am proud of where I am now and there's a pep in my step these days, I will never stop fighting to be better than I was the day before. I don't believe I'll ever be "done" with the work of becoming, and on my deathbed, I intend to ask myself: "Did I make steps towards my happiness and peace, no matter what?" I will be satisfied if I can answer: "Yes."

For most of the last several decades, I found myself frantically searching for a place to lay my heartache down. To pass it off and wash my hands clean of it. If you've ever been in such a place, you know how heavy it is to carry trauma, depression and/or anxiety - how crushing it is. You're walking through life attached to this thing no one can see but you, and it is literally fucking suffocating you. There is no way to verbalize what's happening to anyone around you, and you're crippled by this unwelcome guest. You're cowered there, covering your pain - desperate for help but not wanting to be seen. It is horrible, awful stuff to push through, and I hate it for all of us. The biggest lesson I learned, though, was one that no one could've told me, I just had to come to learn it on my own:

You can never put your trauma down and walk away free from it, but talking about it lightens the load a bit. You and your trauma are one in the same. It does not have to define you, but it is, unfortunately, woven into your fibers and helps define how you move through the world. Only you get to choose if you use it for greater good or succumb to it until it becomes a toxic trait - that is your power and one that cannot be ripped from you, no matter what.

The challenge I would like to see you extend yourself is to learn to walk side by side with your pain. Moving forward looks like whatever you yourself deem. But moving *on* is simply removing the power your past has over you. As you move forward, you are meant to take the pieces of your past that shaped who you are and become more inspired because of them as you create your future. Not all wounds are meant to be healed over completely and forgotten. Be aware of how your trauma shaped you WHILE choosing to live well in spite of it.

If you are feeling lost, that's OK. Just know that you are not alone. If you cannot be convinced that you, too, have a purpose, I ask you: "When do you feel most confident and alive? What are you doing when you feel your spirit buzzing?" That is *your* purpose, and the only way to put your purpose into practice is by stepping into your fear and being steadfast in your vulnerability, even when your heart is cold with anxiety. I'm not saying you have to be fearless, only that you have to go forward through your fear. That's where gods/masters/kings and queens are made.

And so I leave you with one final question my friends, What is *your* purpose?

Made in the USA
Middletown, DE
17 June 2021